Soun Tetoken

NEZ PERCE BOY

Ken Thomasma

Eunice Hundley, *Illustrator*

Baker Book House

Grand Rapids, Michigan 49506

ISBN: **paper:** 0-8010-8873-9
      cloth: 0-8010-8874-7

First printing, June 1984
Second printing, July 1984
Third printing, October 1985

Printed in the United States of America

To

Jim Scott,
of Scott's Horse Palace,
Jackson Hole, Wyoming.

The boys and girls
of Kelly Elementary School, Kelly, Wyoming,
for being good helpers
with the final writing of this book.

Vernon Waters
and
Blanche Waters,
direct descendants
of Old Chief Joseph and his son, Ollokot.

The Nez Perce people
for their hospitality
at the Looking Glass Pow Wow
in August 1983.

Contents

Preface

Soun Tetoken is a fictional character who lives as a typical Nez Perce boy of the Wallowa band would have lived in the 1870s. In this story Soun becomes the adopted son of Ollokot. Ollokot was the son of Old Chief Joseph (Tu-eka-kas) and the brother of Young Chief Joseph, all of whom did live at that time. Neither Young Joseph nor Ollokot had a son the age of Soun. However, the fictional character, Soun, learns many skills from these great Nez Perce leaders and follows their teachings about love and concern for their people. From Soun's experiences the reader also learns their teachings.

Soun is unable to speak. (The description of his disability is medically accurate.) Soun's handicap causes him to rely on his other senses and to develop and strengthen his personal characteristics. He lives with and overcomes his handicap in classic ways. His use of the international Indian sign language is meant to help the reader appreciate the signing skill used by native Americans throughout the centuries.

Soun's friend, Jonas, was also a member of the Wallowa band. He actually lived at that time. Ollokot's daughter, Sarah, married Edward Conner. They had a daughter, Blanche.

Vernon Waters

Blanche Waters

Blanche. Blanche married and had a son, Vernon Waters. Both Vernon and Blanche helped with the research for this book. They both speak fluent Nez Perce and are active in Nez Perce affairs in Idaho and Oregon. Vernon was especially helpful in explaining customs of the Nez Perce and in giving insights into the personality and incidents in the life of young Jonas.

There are many accounts about the historical events in the 1870s, and the details in these accounts differ. In writing about these events, I have been as accurate as possible.

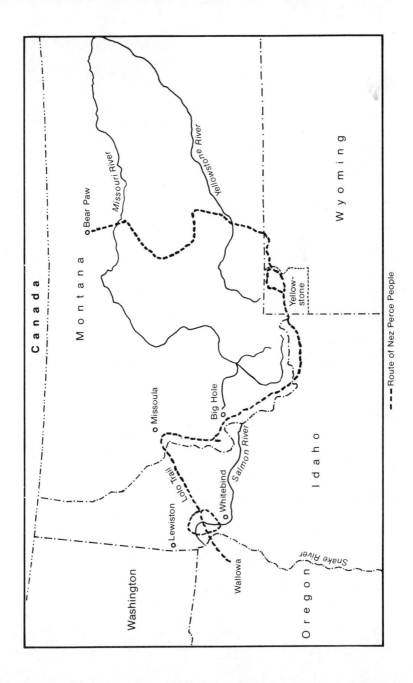

1

Summer Festival

The clear blue mountain lake looked like a giant mirror. Not a ripple stirred its quiet surface. Snowcapped mountain peaks were reflected perfectly in the quiet water. Nearby an Indian village was just as still and quiet except for one small boy who crawled silently from his lodge into the cool morning air. He stood straining his eyes to see in the darkness. The sky above the eastern mountains was just beginning to show a faint promise of daylight.

This boy was much too restless to sleep, for this was the day he had awaited for a long time. It was time to leave for the root-digging festival. Every summer many bands of Nez Perce Indians gathered at favorite places where the meadows lay thick with ripe camas plants.

There would be plenty of excitement for every boy and girl, every man and woman. Along with digging the delicious roots, they would spend plenty of time in games, horse racing, campfires, storytelling, and special dances. Everyone would take his very best clothes, saddles, and blankets on this trip. Jewelry made of beads, porcupine quills, bones, shells, claws, and animal teeth would be worn and traded.

The excitement was enough to keep this small Indian boy from sleeping. But Soun Tetoken had an extra reason for feeling even more excited. Today he would ride on the same horse with his beloved grandfather, the chief. A great stallion would be theirs to ride together. A colorful blanket and tack decorated with beads, quills, and braided horsehair would make the stallion look spectacular.

The boy's grandfather was Chief Tu-eka-kas, now old and blind. He needed his grandson to be his "eyes" for the long ride to the camas prairie. These exciting thoughts filled this six-year-old's mind and made his whole body tingle with nervous energy.

As the sky brightened, suddenly the silence was broken by the call of the Sun Herald who rode his horse slowly through the sleeping village.

"I wonder if everyone is up! It is morning! We are alive, so thanks be! Rise up! Look about! Go see the horses, lest a wolf has killed one! Thanks be that the children are alive! and you, older men! and you, older women!—also that your friends are alive in other camps! Rise up, for a new day has begun!"

While the Sun Herald called his morning greeting, the small boy was already nearing a high place on the ridge above the village. He could see a herd of horses grazing on the sweet summer grass far out on the wide meadow. Looking

back down at the village, he watched women stirring the embers of the past evening's fires. Soon many fires were aglow with flames leaping into the chilly morning air.

In minutes the village was full of activity. Women roasted salmon and trout on long willow sticks. The willow branches were driven into the ground around the fire. The weight of the fish on the end of each stick caused the stick to bend in toward the fire. Soon the air was filled with the smell of roasting fish. Kouse roots cooked in water with other wild vegetables made a delicious soup. It would be a tasty morning meal.

Many of the older boys and men went for a swim in the cold mountain lake. They warmed themselves by the fires and then left to catch horses hobbled near the village. Rawhide hobbles had been tied loosely on the horses' lower legs the night before. The hobbles kept the horses from going too far from the village and made it easier to catch the horses each morning. Once the hobbles were removed, the men and boys mounted their eager animals and rode off toward the main herd in the great meadow.

Skillfully the riders moved around the quietly grazing herd. Half of the riders circled to the left, the other half to the right. In minutes the two lines of riders met and formed a large half-circle around four hundred head of horses. Slowly the riders closed their circle. As they did, the majestic animals raised their heads. They looked at the approaching riders and turned their ears to catch every sound.

Immediately the air was filled with the calls of the alerted horses. The shrill neighing and whinnying caused the riders' horses to answer back as they pranced excitedly. The herd had stopped grazing and slowly gathered closer to each other.

Calmly the riders moved the herd as the first direct rays

14

of sunlight peeked over the eastern mountains. As the animals neared the village, men and boys walked slowly into the herd to catch and tie each horse. These horses were needed to carry the Indian people and their belongings to the root-digging grounds.

The boy who had watched all this moved carefully and calmly toward a great white stallion. The splendid animal looked down at the small lad coming toward him. The stallion turned his head and stood quietly. The boy did not hesitate but skillfully tossed a rawhide loop over the great horse's head. At the same time his small hand stroked the animal's smooth shoulder. The stallion lowered his head and nudged the boy gently.

After the horses were caught and tied, the Indians took time to enjoy the roast fish and kouse soup. As the people finished this fine meal, packing for their trip began. Only a few families would stay behind to care for the rest of the horses, the cattle, and the villagers' property. Everyone else would soon mount their horses to begin the three-day ride to the camas meadow at Weippe.

Old Chief Tu-eka-kas sat quietly by his campfire as everyone packed. He remembered the days when he was a boy, eager and ready for a great trip with his family. His thoughts were interrupted by the sound of running feet.

"Is that you, Soun Tetoken?" asked the blind chief. A single tap on the old man's shoulder was the answer. The chief's grandson could answer him only with a touch. Since the boy had been barely a year old, he was unable to speak or make any sound. He could answer only with sign language.

Soun had been born healthy and normal. At the beginning of his second year of life, his parents were killed in a raging forest fire started by a flash of lightning. Soun was saved

15

by his mother as she sheltered him from the heat with her own body. From that time on the child was unable to make a sound. He was given the name *Soun Tetoken,* which means Silent One. He was adopted immediately by Ollokot, a son of Chief Tu-eka-kas.

When the old chief became blind, he could not read Soun's sign language, so the two of them worked out a way to talk to each other. Grandfather would ask a question. The boy would answer by tapping the chief once for yes and twice for no. Sometimes Soun would sign a message to his father, and Ollokot would tell the blind chief what the boy had said with his signs.

Before the chief became blind, he often had taken Soun for rides high up into the mountains. As soon as the lad was old enough to understand, his grandfather talked to him about being brave, honest, and good to everyone he would meet in his lifetime. Soun's grandfather taught him how to ride, how to take care of his horse, and how to do many other things. It is the Nez Perce custom for grandfathers and grandmothers to care for the children and to teach them how to live good lives.

Many times Soun heard about his grandfather's days at the white man's mission at Lapwai. There Chief Tu-eka-kas learned about the book the white man called the Bible. The white man said the book came from the Great Spirit. Tu-eka-kas learned about Jesus, the son of the Great Spirit, who was sent to earth to teach all men to love each other and to live in peace always.

Chief Tu-eka-kas was a young man when he was baptized by the white missionary, Henry Spalding. The chief was given the name *Joseph* from the Bible. Chief Joseph stayed at the mission station near the Clearwater River for many months. He lived in a tipi with his young wife. He even helped the Reverend Spalding tell more Nez Perce people about Jesus.

Soun and all the Nez Perce children loved to hear these fascinating stories over and over again around the campfire. They could sit for hours and listen to the storytellers speak of the great adventures of the past.

"Is my horse caught and tied, Soun? Is my brave grandson ready to be my 'eyes' for our long journey?" The old chief rose slowly as the boy tapped once after each question.

Old Chief Joseph took the boy's small hand in his, and together they walked over to the beautiful stallion. Soun handed his grandfather the saddle and watched as his grandfather took it from him and put it on the stallion perfectly without being able to see the horse or its saddle. Soun watched the wrinkled hands work quickly and without a slip.

"My son, someday you will be tall and strong. Your body will be full of strength. Your legs will carry you over mountains and through valleys. Your lungs will give you breath to run many miles. Your arms will be strong for fishing and hunting. Your mind will learn the ways of men and the habits of animals. You will learn about the good earth, and how it can take care of you."

The old chief talked as the small boy at his side listened to every word. Despite the noise of the whole village packing for the journey, Soun did not miss a word his grandfather had spoken. Soun had become a better listener than most children. Because he could not speak, he spent more time listening and thinking. He also learned to see things other children missed. He knew the special tricks of most of the horses in the village herd. He knew every dog and how it behaved. Soun loved to watch and study the animals.

When the packing was nearly finished, the Indian families began to line up their horses near the road that would lead them out of the high mountain valley. The warm sun was high above the ridge when the people began to mount their horses. Small children were tied into their saddles. Mothers carried their babies on their backs in cradleboards. Everyone was dressed in his most colorful clothing. There were plenty of horses to carry all the people and their belongings.

It was a spectacular sight to see almost the whole village population dressed in their finest and riding their majestic horses along the trail above Wallowa Lake. The sparkling lake was surrounded by lush green grass sprinkled with wildflowers of every color. Towering snowcapped peaks lined the south and west sides of the lake. Every summer for many years the Nez Perce people lived peacefully in this beautiful valley.

At the front of the long line of riders walked a beautiful stallion with his head held high and his ears turned forward. Old Chief Joseph and his small grandson sat straight and tall in the buckskin saddle. Next to them rode Ollokot on one side and his brother Hin-mah-too-yah-lat-kekht on the other side. Soun's uncle would become the chief when old Joseph died.

The old chief talked to his two sons as they rode out of sight of their village. "My sons, I feel that this is my last trip away from this valley that I have loved so much these many summers of my life. When we return, we must prepare for the day I shall leave you to go to be with the Great Spirit Chief. You are both good sons. You have done much to make your old father happy and proud. You have already been a great help to our people. You must never let your own desires stand in the way of your duty to serve our many brothers and sisters and their children. Remember the old people in their days of need. Soon our people will depend on you to be wise and honest as you guide our village as leaders."

Soun sat listening to his grandfather's words. He watched his father and his uncle as they rode next to him. He saw their serious faces and noticed how closely they were listening to their blind father. Soun did not understand all that was said, but he knew the words carried a serious message with some sadness.

As the riders came over a rise in the trail, a rail fence came into view. Beyond the fence cattle grazed. In a clump of trees near a small stream a canvas tent could be seen. Behind the tent the sound of an ax hitting wood rang out in the clear morning air. Soon the chopping stopped, and the face of a white man appeared at the edge of the trees. He stood quietly and watched the Nez Perce people pass.

As the old chief and his sons rode past, they talked about the *so-ya-po* (white man), and how many of them were coming into the Wallowa Valley and taking land. They talked about the white man's fences, his plows, his fields of grain, and his strange ways of living. Mostly they talked about the white man and his councils with the Nez Perce on the Clearwater River. They talked about promises and treaties broken by the so-ya-po. Yes, many of the white men could not be trusted. Many of their words were lies. They even argued about Jesus and the Great Spirit. The old chief talked about living his own life without the white man's help.

The chief and his sons talked most of the morning. Time passed quickly. Soon all the riders stopped for a rest in a large meadow. A clear cold stream was a good place to drink. The people could stretch and rest here before going farther down the trail toward the Snake River.

After a brief afternoon thunderstorm, the weather cleared. The evening camp was made near a stand of aspen trees at the base of a steep ridge. Most of the people would sleep in the open, covered with their blankets as they lay on beds of grass and pine boughs spread over hides.

Soun's mother, Fair Land, and three other women worked quickly with poles, rawhide rope, and large hides. They built a fine tipi for Old Chief Joseph. Soun and the other boys cared for the horses. Saddles, blankets, and bridles were carefully laid over logs or hung from the low branches of nearby trees.

The campsite was a good one with water, plenty of firewood, and lots of fine grass for the horses. This same campsite was used each summer that the Wallowa Nez Perce traveled this way.

Boys aged six to twelve worked as herders. While the camp was being set up, the boys rode the sidehills, watching the horses below. The boys were alert for signs of roaming wolf packs, for traces of prowling mountain lions, and even for the chance of seeing the great grizzly bear.

Nez Perce boys were well trained to read animal signs. Tracks, droppings, a bit of fur, a broken twig, a place where an animal had lain down, all were clues. From these signs Indian boys could tell an important story. Just one sign left by a wild animal could tell the boy what kind of animal had been at this place, how long ago it had been there, the size of the animal, and even if there had been more than one animal in the area.

The boys traveled in a large circle around the horses. They looked carefully for signs of danger to the herd. While they worked, older boys and men were out hunting game. Moose, elk, deer, mountain sheep, antelope, and bear were their favorite game animals. Moose and elk were the animals easiest to find in the high mountains during summer months. One of these large animals would give enough delicious meat to feed many people.

Soun often dreamed of the day when he too would be able to hunt the great animals. Many of the games Nez Perce boys played helped them with their hunting skills. Running races, shooting bow and arrow made with their own hands, wrestling to test their strength, and even horse racing trained the boys to be good hunters. However, on this day there was no time for games. Campfires were banked early. The people would be up at dawn to prepare to continue their journey.

After two more days of travel and the safe crossing of three large rivers, the Wallowa band of Nez Perce climbed a winding trail to the high camas prairie at Weippe. In the trees at the edge of this wide prairie were the tipis of hundreds of Nez Perce people. Children were playing, women were cooking or putting up tipis, men were greeting each other and planning horse races. Boys took the horses off to good grazing areas on the hillsides and meadows above the camas prairie. They took turns watching the herds. Girls were busy preparing the root-digging sticks for the next day's work. They sharpened old sticks and made new ones to replace worn tools.

As Soun and his grandfather rode through all this activity, the boy's eyes and ears took it all in. Everyone they passed greeted Old Chief Joseph with words of great respect. Soun felt proud to be on the same horse with his famous grandfather.

Soon the Wallowa Nez Perce arrived at their campsite. Everyone knew what work had to be done and set to the tasks quickly. Soun unsaddled the big stallion and rode him bareback to the meadow high above the camp. Soun released the horse and walked along the ridge, looking for signs of danger to the herd.

Soun usually did his work alone. Because he was unable to speak except with sign language, other boys did not take time to talk to him. Soun learned to use his ears and eyes well because he spent very little time "talking" with his hands.

Soun finished his walk around the horses and made his way through the fir trees and down the hillside to the camp. Everyone was busy. Even three-year-old children were expected to do a little work. Tipis were going up. Some were covered with woven mats and some were covered with hides sewn together. Girls and women gathered large amounts of firewood. Water containers made from animal skins were filled and hung from trees. Soon a comfortable camp was all set up and ready to be lived in and enjoyed during the five-day festival.

That night there was a great ceremonial campfire. The best dancers from each band did an exciting dance in their colorful costumes. Chiefs from each band gave a short speech of welcome to all the people there. Each chief thanked the Great Spirit Chief for another good crop of delicious camas roots. Each chief asked all Nez Perce to work and play hard and greet each other in peace and love.

The campfire lasted long into the night. It was exciting and time passed quickly. Even the smallest children stayed awake, not missing a single dance and listening to every word spoken.

2

A Day of Adventure

For five days the women and children would dig the precious camas roots and store them in woven baskets lined with bark and grass. The boys watched the horses and exercised the animals that would be raced by the men. Every afternoon braves raced their fastest horses against those from other bands. Many bets were made on each race.

Soun loved to watch the strong braves dressed in breechcloths and knee-high moccasins mount their horses and race off in a cloud of dust. Each rider leaned far forward over his horse's neck, urging his animal on to greater and greater speed. Horses would strain forward, every muscle flexing for more power and speed.

The Nez Perce were the best horse breeders and trainers of all the Indian people that Lewis and Clark met in their great expedition from Saint Louis to the Pacific Ocean. The Nez Perce used only the finest stallions to sire their herds. They had large herds with as many as seven to ten horses for every man, woman, and child. All children learned to ride almost as soon as they could sit up alone. Horses were traded with the white man for many things the Indian wanted.

When the third day of the festival came, two things happened that Soun would always remember. The Nez Perce people would talk about this day around their campfires for many years.

As usual Soun was up early and eager to climb the hillside to check the horses before it was time for the morning meal. A few women were uncovering the hot coals and adding wood to build up the flames. A few boys were out and on their way to check their horses.

Soun moved up the hillside through the trees and onto an open slope. He could see the horses grazing in the distance and below him. Some of the animals had moved up the hill in the early morning shade. Something seemed a little different to Soun as he walked farther along and up the ridge above the horses. He noticed that the horses below all moved quickly away from the hill. Something was wrong.

As Soun neared a small clump of trees and bushes, he saw some movement below and to his left. There was an outcropping of rock at that spot. He hurried around the stunted trees for a better view. Below him a filly stood on the edge of the protruding rocks. Her mother was below her and separated from her by the steep rocks. They were desperately trying to get back together.

It didn't look like a serious problem. Colts and fillies were

often separated from the mares for a short time, but they usually got back together quickly. Soun watched for only a short time and decided he would circle around from above and move the filly back to her mother.

Soun had taken only a few steps away from the trees when he saw a movement on a rock above the small horse. He looked more closely. It was a large mountain lion whose color helped it blend in with the rock. The big cat had seen the filly get separated from her mother and was moving in for the kill.

Instantly Soun started moving to a place right above the two animals. The lion did not see or hear the boy. The mountain lion was ready to spring upon the helpless filly. Soun had no weapon except the knife in his belt. He needed to think fast to help the small horse. Soun worked to loosen some medium-sized rocks. As he worked, the powerful cat sprang from his rock in a silent graceful leap. Soun saw the mighty cat hit the filly and knock her down onto the rocks.

Quickly Soun pushed two of the larger rocks down the hillside toward the fallen animals. The rolling rocks loosened other rocks and a small avalanche started down the hill. In seconds the falling rocks reached the mountain lion and the filly. Most of the rocks missed the animals by several feet. They did scare the cat away from the filly long enough for Soun to come slipping and sliding down the hill. On his way down Soun grabbed a large stick. The filly had scrambled to her feet. When the dust cleared, the mountain lion was again poised and ready to leap. Quickly Soun stepped between the lion and the filly. He raised his stick and waved it wildly. The big cat snarled and pawed at the air in anger. All this time the mother of the filly reared on her hind legs and neighed loudly. The mare kicked at the rocks on the

26

ledge below as if she wanted to climb the wall to save her young one.

All this commotion attracted the attention of two boys who were riding their horses a good distance away. They hurried to a place where they could see what all the fuss was about. When they saw a small boy holding off a mountain lion with only a stick, they could hardly believe their eyes. Immediately they started their horses running toward Soun. They hollered loudly as they rode at top speed. That was all it took to convince the lion that it was time to leave. The big cat scampered straight up the hill and disappeared into the trees.

When the two older boys got to Soun, he had already checked the filly. She had suffered only a few cuts from the cat's sharp claws. The cuts on the filly's neck and back would heal. The two older boys still could not believe that this small boy had dared to take on a mountain lion with only a stick. Not knowing that Soun could not speak, the two boys started asking him questions one right after another.

With sign language that all Indian people understood, Soun told the boys that he could not speak. Then with his hands he told the boys exactly what had happened. As they talked, they walked the filly back to her anxious mother. The mare nuzzled the filly and began to lick the cuts on her neck and back.

When the boys returned to the camp, the word spread quickly about the attack on the filly and how Soun had acted quickly and bravely to save the young horse's life. Old Chief Joseph greeted his young grandson warmly and repeatedly told him how proud he was of him. Many people came by to see the brave six-year-old and said kind things to Soun. All the boys were told to watch for the lion's return. After

27

what had happened to that cat, he probably would not be back soon.

This was not the end of the excitement for the day. That same afternoon Soun's father, Ollokot, was in a horse race that would be talked about at campfires for years to come.

Soun was watching with great excitement as his father got ready for the big race. This would be one of the best races of the festival. Ollokot would be competing against the finest riders and fastest horses from all the other villages. Most of the other riders were sons of Nez Perce chiefs also.

One chief was sure his son would win. He offered six fine horses as a bet on his son. Chief Joseph quickly agreed to match the bet and had six of his horses brought over. Many men had bets on this race. They offered horses, buffalo hides, fine jewelry, knives, and feathers.

Ollokot was a fine rider. His horse was one of the swiftest in the Wallowa herd of more than three thousand horses. This long-legged stallion had won many races in the past. Ollokot would do his best to win this one, too.

The riders would travel once around a small hill on the east side of the great camas prairie. The race would follow a well-worn road. The finish was in front of the main campfire area. Everyone would be waiting eagerly to see the leaders come racing in.

The excited riders mounted their beautiful horses and began to bring the nervous animals up to the starting line. Soun watched his father skillfully guide his mount toward the start. He saw the muscles in his father's arms and legs strain as he rode into position. Ollokot's skin glistened in the sunlight as sweat poured from his body.

A brave stood off to one side and in front of the tense riders. The man held up a long staff which was decorated with bright paint and dangling feathers. It seemed as if he held the staff up for a long time. The nervous horses pranced and threw their heads up and down. They strained forward, eager to begin running.

Suddenly the brave pulled the staff to the earth, and the race had begun. A great cloud of dust arose as the horses' churning hooves dug in for a fast start. The riders urged their mounts on, trying to gain a good position early in the race. Many people moved to higher ground for a better view of the race.

When the dust cleared, Ollokot could be seen running fourth early in the race. He knew he could catch and pass the three leaders easily before the finish. He was watching the rider behind him very carefully. This was Two Moons, a great rider, on a great stallion. He was the one to beat.

Ollokot held his position, waiting for the right moment to pass the leaders. He must make his move before Two Moons could pass him, but not too soon or his horse might tire before the finish and lose to Two Moons.

The horses were running hard with their riders leaning far over their necks. None of the first six racers was far from the leader. The riders had rounded the small hill and were making the long run back to the finish line when Ollokot decided to make his move. He had waited as long as he dared. Quickly Ollokot pulled his horse to the outside to pass the three riders in front of him. Two Moons followed right on Ollokot's heels and was coming on fast.

As Ollokot moved up alongside the horse running in third place, he saw a terrible thing happen directly in front of him. The leading horse suddenly stumbled and fell to the ground. The rider sailed forward, hit the ground, and rolled over several times.

It all happened so fast that Ollokot, Two Moons, and the other riders were past the fallen horse and rider in an instant. Ollokot just caught a glimpse of the face of the fallen man, a face covered with dirt and blood. Without another thought, Ollokot pulled his horse to the left and out of the race. The other racers rode on to the finish line. Ollokot rode back to the fallen rider, who lay unconscious and bleeding.

Ollokot quickly covered an open wound on the man's scalp with his hands and pressed hard to stop the bleeding. The blood oozed from beneath his hands, but it had already started coming out more slowly. Ollokot looked up and saw help coming. He didn't notice Soun standing on a small knoll behind him, watching as his father gave aid to the injured man. Several people came up on horseback. Others came running to offer help and to see what had happened.

A stretcher was hurriedly made from two long poles and a large hide. The hide was stretched between the poles and fastened tightly. As soon as Ollokot had stopped the bleeding, four strong braves carried the injured man on the stretcher to the camp. The man's wounds were cleaned and wrapped. Cold water was carefully poured over his head and face to revive him. He would recover from his injuries.

The race was easily won by Two Moons, but when the people saw how Ollokot had stopped to save the injured rider, no bets were paid. Everyone knew that Ollokot had done a great thing. Ollokot never thought twice about finishing the race. He thought only of helping a friend who needed him. No race was more important than helping a person in great need.

Old Chief Joseph was very proud of his son and his grandson because of the brave deeds they had done this day. Soun was proud just to stand near his father and listen to the good

30

words the people said to Ollokot after the race. The Nez Perce people admire a person who forgets himself and thinks of others first. This was the lesson the old blind chief had taught his children and grandchildren.

At the campfire that night many people spoke of the things that had happened on this third day of the festival. These stories would be added to all the other great tales that would be told for years to come around campfires all over the Nez Perce lands.

Death of a Great Chief

Following the horse races each day, large meals were prepared and enjoyed by all. There was lots of visiting back and forth between people from all the villages. There were many campfires and plenty of time for storytelling.

Soun loved to play games with all the other Indian boys. Wrestling was great fun. Two boys would stand facing each other. At a signal both boys would charge forward, trying to grab the opponent and knock him down on his back. The boy who could do this two times to his opponent was the winner. Soun was a very good wrestler and was able to defeat most boys his own age and size. He even liked to challenge boys older and bigger than he. Soun ended up with many bruises and bumps, but he was always ready for more action. Soun loved all the games, especially the roughest ones.

The days went quickly, and the root harvest ended with a final big campfire. The trip home was made in mostly rainy weather. The warm and dry lodges at their village in the Wallowa Valley were a welcome sight to the weary travelers. Soun liked trips but was always excited to be home again.

The rest of the summer passed quickly and the aspen trees began to turn a beautiful gold. The Wallowa Nez Perce were busy storing food and getting ready for winter.

That fall the villagers were called together on a sunny morning. They stood quietly waiting for some important news to be given. Soun stood on a tree stump so he could see over the heads of the crowd. He could just see the face of his uncle over all the adults in front of him.

"Brothers and sisters, I come to you with a heavy heart," said the older son of Chief Joseph. "For all my thirty-one summers, I have loved my great and good father. I know that every one of you loves him as a father, also. He has served us well. He shared our happiness. He stood with us in our sadness. He loved his people. He loved this valley and his mother earth. Last night while I held his hand, he left us to begin his journey to the land of the Great Spirit. Our chief, our father, our friend is dead. Let us prepare him for his journey to the Spirit Land."

The people stood in perfect silence after hearing the sad news. Not a single person moved. Soun stood on the tree stump. His head was down. He cried without a sound. Tears streamed down his face and fell at his feet.

As the minutes passed, the followers of Old Chief Joseph began to move slowly away from the meeting place. Soun stepped down and sat on the stump. This was the day of his

birth. Never before had Soun felt as sad as he did on this day. It was only a short time before that his grandfather had told him that the chief's best mare would have a special foal. The mare had been bred with the chief's finest stallion. Old Joseph had told Soun that the foal would be Soun's horse. It would be the first horse the boy could call his very own.

Soun had promised his beloved grandfather that he would take great care to train the horse well and that he would ride it with pride. Soun promised to make his grandfather proud of him in every way. Now Soun sat by himself, very sad and very lonely. His grandfather was gone.

The chief's body was dressed in the finest clothes decorated with beautiful beadwork and jewelry. Around his neck hung necklaces of beautiful shells, elk teeth, bear claws, and polished bone. The chief's face was painted with bright colors according to ancient custom. The body was placed on a platform built about three feet above the ground and located under a giant fir tree. There it would stay until buried two days later.

From the moment the people had left the meeting, women who were close relatives of the chief began to cry out in high-pitched voices. This constant wailing filled the village. All other sounds were muffled. Soun sat motionless that afternoon. He was on a small hill just above the place where his grandfather's body lay. He saw his mother, Fair Land, crying out with the other women as they stood near the body.

It was hard for a seven-year-old boy to know the meaning of death. Soun knew he had lost someone he loved as much as he had ever loved anyone. He spent hours sitting in this same place close to his grandfather's body. Several times he got up and walked to the chief's body. Each time he placed a small gift on the platform. Each gift was from Soun's own

36

collection of feathers, elk teeth, and shells. Soun stood quietly near his grandfather's motionless body and thought how he would gladly give everything he had if his grandfather could be alive again.

Where is the Great Spirit? Is my grandfather's spirit still here in his body or has it already left for the Spirit Land? When I die will my spirit go to see Grandfather and the Great Spirit? What is death? Why do people die? Soun did a lot of thinking as he sat in silence.

Soun was startled as a hand touched his shoulder from behind. He turned and saw his uncle, Hin-mah-too-yah-lat-kekht.

"Soun Tetoken, you loved your grandfather very much. You are sad. I too have a heavy heart. It is proper to be sad. It is good to love a great one like your grandfather. His body lies cold and still. His spirit is gone, but he has left us all something good and beautiful. He has left his wisdom, his love, and his wishes for a good life. Soun, you will be a better man because you had such a noble grandfather. Remember him, his words, his deeds, and his love for you and all his people. If you do, you will become a good man like him. Be sad now, my son, but soon we will go back to live our lives as the great chief lived his."

His uncle's words made Soun feel much better. He knew it was all right to feel sad and lonely. He knew that in a few days his life would go on as before, only without his dear grandfather.

The day of the funeral was a clear sunny October day. The chief's body was wrapped very tightly with soft deerskin. It was laid on a crude stretcher made of many poles tied together. This bier with the chief's body was carried to the grave by four strong braves. All the chief's relatives and friends followed. The men walked in silence while the women cried out loudly all the way.

The four braves slowly lowered the body into the grave which was dug into a rocky hillside. The chief was placed facing east. The women stopped wailing, and all was quiet. The village medicine man spoke a few words about the goodness and great deeds of Chief Tu-eka-kas. Next the chief's sons and daughters dropped many trinkets into the grave. Strips of cedar wood were placed in the grave to cover the body. Then stones were piled on the wood. Finally earth was spread over the grave.

Soun watched and listened. Tears streamed silently down his face. Through the tears he saw the chief's great stallion led to a place near the grave. Soun remembered his happy journey to the root-digging grounds. This stallion was the same horse he had ridden with his grandfather. This stallion had sired the unborn foal that Grandfather said would be his next summer.

Soun watched as men quickly built strong log supports under the great horse's body. Soun knew what was going to happen. He could not watch. Soun turned and ran toward the village. Soon he heard one rifle shot followed quickly by a second one. He knew the big stallion was dead. The horse was killed, as was the custom, so the horse's spirit would be ready to carry Chief Joseph's spirit to its spirit home. The horse would be left standing, held up by the log supports under its body. All these things were so hard for Soun to understand. He would ponder them for many days and years to come.

Soon after the death of Chief Tu-eka-kas, whom the white man called Chief Joseph, a new chief took over the leadership of the Wallowa Nez Perce band. The new chief was Soun's uncle and the son of Tu-eka-kas. The white man would call the new chief Young Chief Joseph. Soun's father, Ollokot, would be a great help to his brother, the new Chief Joseph.

The white settlers were coming in larger numbers every year. They took Nez Perce land in the Wallowa Valley whenever and wherever they wanted it. Old Chief Joseph died on October 5, 1871, and already one white settler had moved in, fenced off a large piece of land, and built a cabin and other buildings. Years before Ollokot and Soun's uncle had helped put painted poles in the ground. These poles marked the land belonging to the Nez Perce people. Soon the whites would come and knock down the poles and begin taking the land.

One month after Old Chief Joseph's death, a great feast was given by the chief's family. Friends came from miles away. Dried fish, fresh elk and moose, biscuits, berries, fruits, and nuts made a delicious meal for all. Because it was November 5, the feast was held in the afternoon. The weather was beautiful. Everyone talked about past adventures and the accomplishments of Chief Tu-eka-kas.

After the feast, Young Chief Joseph rose to speak. Soun watched and listened as his uncle spoke to the crowd. The new chief talked about the goodness of his father, Tu-ela-kas. He told the people about the old chief's last words.

"The night of his death my father sent for me. I took his hand in mine. I saw that he was dying. He said, 'My son, my body is returning to my mother earth, and my spirit is going very soon to see the Great Spirit Chief. When I am gone, think of your country. You are chief of these people. They look to you to guide them. Always remember that your father never sold this land. You must stop up your ears whenever you are asked to sign a treaty selling your home. A few years more and the white men will be all around you. They have their eyes on this land. My son, never forget my dying words. This land holds your father's body. Never sell the bones of your father and mother."[1] I pressed my father's hand and told him I would protect his grave with my life. My father smiled and passed away to the spirit land.

"My brothers and sisters, I promise you, I will never sell this valley. I will keep the promise I made to my father. I also promise to help you, my people. I will love the children and live in peace with all men.

"Now my family has gifts for all of you. My father wished that each of you have something from his belongings as a gift of love from him."

Soun watched as his father and mother, his uncle, and his aunts passed out many fine gifts to all their friends and relatives. These gifts were things owned by the great Chief Tu-eka-kas. It was a happy time with everyone expressing their thanks and wishing the family of Young Chief Joseph good health and long life.

As Soun stood next to his step-sister, Sarah, he thought about the exciting gift his grandfather had given him before his death. That gift would come in June when a beautiful mare would give birth to a foal. The foal would be Soun's very own, to raise, to train, and to ride proudly.

With sign language Soun told Sarah that he was thinking about the day he would see his gift from their grandfather.

"Soun, you will have a fine horse. Grandfather will look down from his spirit home and smile on the day your foal is born," said Sarah.

1. Quoted in Alvin M. Josephy, Jr., *The Nez Perce Indians and the Opening of the Northwest* (New Haven: Yale University Press, 1965), p. 442.

With fast-moving hands Soun answered, "I will remember Grandfather every day. I will grow to be a good and brave man like him. I hope to make his spirit happy by remembering his words and his deeds. I will ride my horse with great happiness."

These were big thoughts for young children, but Indian children had to grow up quickly. At age three Nez Perce boys and girls learned to help gather food. Grandmothers taught the little ones how to pick berries, gather seeds and nuts, and dig roots. Soun and Sarah had already become good workers for their family. They had learned many important lessons that would help them live useful lives.

All the gifts had been given and most of the people were getting ready for the ceremonial dancing. Soun and Sarah looked up to see the new Chief Joseph coming toward them. The chief had a loving smile on his face.

"My children, you have not been forgotten. Soun, your grandfather loved you with all his heart. In June you will receive your own horse, a gift from him. Take this bridle which your grandfather used as he rode many miles through this land that he loved. Use it as you, also, ride straight in the saddle on your own horse. Remember the hands of him who held this bridle before you. Those hands did much to care for me, for your father, for you, and for all our people. Your hands can do great things, also."

As the chief spoke, Soun felt a shiver go through his whole body. He felt as though he could not stand still. He wanted to begin that very moment to work for his people. He wanted to prove that he had learned the great lessons of life that his grandfather had taught him.

Soun hardly heard the words the chief spoke as he gave his daughter a beautiful beaded bag that had belonged to her grandfather. As Young Chief Joseph turned and brought small gifts to the other grandchildren, Soun and Sarah rushed off with their treasures. They would both remember this day for the rest of their lives. They would remember the words spoken. They would prize their gifts. Most of all they would remember their loving grandfather.

A Special Foal Is Born

The day after the great feast and gift giving, the Wallowa Nez Perce began to pack for their journey to their winter home in the valley of the Imnaha River. The days were shorter now. The mountain meadows were often frost-covered in the morning. Several times the people woke up to snow on the ground. The great elk had stopped bugling. The leaf-bearing trees had dropped all their leaves. It was time to move to the valley before the deep snows came to the Wallowa.

That winter there was a good supply of dried game meat and smoked fish. There were plenty of roots, berries, seeds, fruits, and nuts stored in woven baskets. All the work done during the spring, summer, and fall months would provide the Nez Perce families with enough food to last the whole winter.

During the winter days the men went on snowshoes to hunt game in the high valleys. They also spent lots of time making arrow and spear points from black glasslike rock called obsidian. The women were busy every day making baskets, tanning hides, preparing meals, and sewing clothing from animal skins. The hides of even the smallest animals were used to make articles of clothing. Women also took time to fashion jewelry and to do beautiful beadwork.

Darkness came early and winter nights were long. There was plenty of time for stories around the fires in the lodges. The children loved to hear their favorite tales over and over again.

Soun's favorite story was the legend that told where people came from. The legend tells about a huge sea monster named Ilts-wet-six that roamed the Kamiah Valley. The monster was so large and so hungry that he had come out of the sea and was soon eating all the animals of the land. When Coyote heard what the monster was doing, he decided to do something about it. Coyote came to the Kamiah Valley and tied himself to the earth with a strong grapevine. Coyote called out to the giant Ilts-wet-six to try to eat him. The monster came and sucked and sucked until finally the grapevine came loose, and Coyote was pulled into the monster's stomach. However, Coyote had not lost the battle yet. He had a knife hidden in his belt. He took the knife and cut out the sea monster's heart, killing the great beast. Next Coyote used the knife to cut his way out of the monster's body.

Fox had watched the battle. When Coyote could not de-

cide what to do with the monster's body, Fox said, "Cut up the whole body and make people from its parts."

So from the head of the monster came the Flathead Indians, from the feet came the Blackfoot people, and from each part of the body a different Indian nation. In the end only the heart was left. Coyote lifted it high above the ground. More people sprang up from the blood dripping from the beast's heart. These people were taller, stronger, kinder, and wiser than all the others. These were the Nez Perce people.

The Great Spirit Chief, who rules the whole earth, was well pleased by Coyote's victory and work. The Great Spirit Chief did not want the Nez Perce to forget what Coyote had done, so he took the monster's heart and turned it into a large rock. This rock can still be seen in the Kamiah Valley.

Every time Soun heard the sound of a coyote he remembered this famous Nez Perce legend. On this night when he heard the legend again, springtime was near. After the story was finished, Soun lay down on his buffalo robe and went to sleep.

The first salmon to come up the Imnaha River signaled the beginning of serious fishing. Soon the salmon and trout would come by the thousands on their spawning runs. In many places the fish would be so thick that men could dip them out with nets. Fish traps were built on narrow channels of the river. A temporary dam was made at the upper end of the channel. Rocks were used to narrow the channel from each side. Then sticks were used to close the gap while still letting water flow through. As the big fish swam upstream into the trap and it filled with fish, the fishermen quickly closed off the lower end of the channel with a gate made of sticks woven and tied together. The gate fit perfectly into the opening, blocking the fishes' escape.

Then the men dipped the fish out by the hundreds with their nets. On the riverbank women and children cleaned the large fish and cut them in half. Some of the meat could be roasted, some was put on drying racks, and some was smoked in special underground pits. When the trout and salmon runs were on, everyone caught and processed fish from dawn until dark. Fishing was so good that each Nez Perce could eat an average of more than one pound of fish a day, every day of the year.

Fresh fish roasted over an open fire was a great treat after a long winter of eating mainly smoked or dried meat. Kouse roots were the first fresh roots of spring and also tasted delicious.

For Soun the spring of 1872 held the promise of the birth of his long-awaited foal. All during the winter, he watched the beautiful mare as she grazed with the other horses in the valley near the waters of the Imnaha River. Soun was anxious for the day the villagers would start up the trail to the Wallowa Valley.

Hunters who had gone out during the winter in search of game returned and told of finding very little snow in the high valleys. That made game hard to find. The animals spread out more and did not need to come into the valleys to escape the snow. It also meant that the people could return to their summer home a little earlier than usual.

All of the fish caught that spring was packed along with a good supply of fresh kouse roots. Hides, clothing, tools, and all the villagers' belongings were prepared for the journey to the Wallowa.

Soun had grown taller over the winter. He felt a great surge of excitement as he caught a hobbled horse and rode off to help round up the horses and cattle for the trip up the trail. The route followed a creek swollen with spring run-off water. The trail led up the canyon and was in the trees part of the time and on open sidehills part of the way.

It wasn't a long trip, but the people took their time. There were good places to dig roots along the way, and many days were taken to reach the Wallowa Valley. It was an exciting time, especially for the boys and girls. They loved to travel and camp along the way.

When the people arrived in the valley, they found that the lake was still frozen. There were only a few places where there was open water. There were still banks of snow where the direct rays of the sun could not reach and melt them. The great mountains were covered with snow.

Soun rode near the herd of horses, helping keep the thousands of animals moving in the right direction. He looked at all the familiar sights on the way through the high valley. It was a warm sunny day. The grass was a deep green. Early spring flowers were in bloom. The ground was moist. The smells of spring were everywhere. It was exciting to be back.

A lot of work was waiting for the Wallowa Nez Perce villagers as they rode up to their summer homesites. Stored lodge poles were taken and put up on familiar ground. Mats and hides were carefully placed over the poles so rain and snow would shed without allowing a drop to enter the lodges. Firepits were rebuilt. Racks for drying meat were taken out of storage and repaired. Pine boughs and grasses were gathered to place under hides to make warm and comfortable beds.

Everyone had work to do and all were happy and excited about their return to their beautiful valley. Soun rode a horse over a familiar trail as he watched the hungry herd of horses and cattle feed on the tender, sweet spring grass. The mare he had watched so closely all winter grazed just below him.

Soun stopped his horse and took a careful look around the open meadows. He noticed how large the mare looked. Her sides bulged. It wouldn't be long now before the foal would be born. Soun planned to watch the mare during every spare minute he had.

The summer of 1872 would bring events that would soon change the life of every Wallowa Nez Perce. Many white men would come and take Nez Perce land for their own. They were already living in many places in the valley— building fences, cabins, and farm buildings.

Soun heard his father, his uncle, Young Chief Joseph, and the other village leaders talk about the white settlers and how to get them to stop taking Nez Perce land. Some of the younger men wanted to drive the white men out with weapons. Others favored telling the settlers to leave or face death if they refused. Young Chief Joseph listened to everyone. He said he would have a council with the whites and ask them to leave in peace.

Soun was troubled by the words he heard, but he forgot all of this on his trips away from the village to check on the horses. This was the time for birth in the herd. Several mares had already had their foals.

On a cold rainy morning Soun was up early as usual. He ate dried salmon and two kouseroot biscuits. He ate quickly and was on his way to see the horses and find the big mare.

Soun kept moving to stay warm on this chilly, damp morning. It took him a long time to find the mare. It was the middle of the morning when Soun found her near a small grove of trees. She was not grazing and stood quietly near the trees, looking straight ahead.

49

Soun had an extra robe of hide to put over his shoulders to help shed the cold drizzle. He found a place where he could crawl under the overhanging branches of a large fir tree. Soun sat down on the dry needles under the tree and watched the mare.

The beautiful horse moved very little as time passed slowly. Many thoughts went through Soun's mind as he sat quietly. He thought about the day he sat next to his grandfather and heard him promise the gift of his very own horse. Would this be the day his foal would be born? Would it be a colt or a filly? Would the foal be strong and healthy? What color would it be?

As Soun daydreamed, time seemed to pass very slowly. Suddenly he forgot about time. The mare began to move about a little. She started breathing quite hard. It was time for her to give birth.

Soun was only fifty feet away as he watched closely. The mare moved under the branches of a nearby tree to get out of the cold rain. Soon she knelt down and lay on her left side. Her breathing became faster.

Soun forgot about the cold and the rain as he watched anxiously. The big mare raised her head several times and looked back as if to see her foal. Each time her head went back to the ground in a resting position. How long Soun sat and watched, he did not know. His great excitement erased the meaning of time.

Then the birth started. Soun watched in amazement as a wet dark form began to protrude from the mare's body. In only seconds the foal's head was out, followed by the forelegs. For a moment the birth seemed to stop, only to begin again until the squirming foal fell free to the ground. The baby horse was very wet and a membrane clung to parts of its body. A little blood could be seen.

Right after the birth, the mare got to her feet and turned to look at her newborn baby. She gently lowered her head and began to lick the foal to clean it and help it get dry. Soun watched all this, unaware of anything else that was happening around him. He didn't even notice the sudden break in the clouds and the sun peeking through the opening. Soun was on his feet, trying to get a better look at the foal. His excitement was the greatest he had ever felt.

Only a few minutes had passed since the birth and already the foal had its head up. Soon it started trying to get its legs underneath its body so it could stand up.

The struggle to stand up was the next part of this fascinating scene. As the foal began to raise itself from the ground for the first time, Soun could see that the newborn was a colt. The frail little fellow was weak, and awkward on his wobbly legs. His body seemed to be too small. He looked like he was all legs, and they were too thin and shaky to support him. His mother nuzzled him and continued to lick him clean.

The foal had been standing only a short time when suddenly his legs seemed to fold up and send him back onto the ground to start the struggle all over again. Once again the foal worked his legs underneath his body. This time it did not take as long for the foal to get to his feet.

With each passing minute the foal became steadier. He kept his legs spread apart to keep his balance. Next he moved a little and was soon poking his head beneath his mother's stomach to begin nursing.

For the first time since the excitement began, Soun took his eyes off this amazing scene. The sun was now shining brightly. The storm clouds had moved east. About a dozen curious horses were standing side by side in a row sniffing the air. They were looking at the new arrival and his mother. When one of the mares got too close, the foal's mother laid her ears back and moved toward the intruder, ready to fight. The curious mare backed away in a hurry.

Soun knew the many dangers to newborn horses. All of these dangers did not come from wild animals. Some of the threats to the foal's life could come from other horses in the herd. A dry mare without a foal might try to take the colt away from his mother. Even a gelding might try to do the same thing. If a horse succeeded in stealing the colt, he could starve to death without his mother's milk.

Soun walked slowly around the trees toward the other horses and chased them off. He would come every day to make sure the foal was safe with his mother. On this special June day the sun had come out at almost the same time the foal was born. Soun thought about this sudden change in the weather as he moved into the warm sunshine for a little closer look at the awkward little horse.

The mare had moved into the sunshine, also, and stood quietly as the foal nursed. The curious horses did not return. They went back to grazing. Soun stayed near the mare and foal for hours. He could see that the colt had beautiful markings. His shoulders and head were a dark gray like his mother. His face was a lighter gray with a bright white spot just above his eyes. Most unusual of all were the beautiful markings on the right hip. There Soun saw a large circle of white with short rags of the white coloring coming out of the circle here and there. It looked much like the sun and its rays of light. The circle of white had black and gray spots large and small sprinkled through it.

As Soun thought about the sudden end of the rain and the coming of the sunshine and the sunlike markings on the foal's hip, he knew what he would name the colt. His name would be Sunburst. No other name would fit this special colt.

Soun was eager for the day to come when he could go close to his colt and even touch him. For now he would have to just watch from a safe distance. The colt needed time to learn about the world from his mother.

It was late in the day when Soun finally returned to the village. He hurried to tell his father the news. Ollokot watched proudly as his son's hands moved quickly and gracefully, telling the whole story of the birth of Sunburst.

"This is a great day for you, Soun Tetoken. Your grandfather loved you greatly. Now he still tells you of his love with this special gift. When it is time, train your colt to obey. Train him to do as you command. Ride with your back straight and your head high. All the days of your life remember the love of your wise and kind grandfather."

The boy listened carefully to the words of his father. He never felt happier. He ate his evening meal quickly and rode a horse back to the meadow to spend two more hours watching the mare and Sunburst.

Soun was up early every morning. He hurried out to the herd to do his work. He checked for any signs of danger to the horses. He could easily pick out the mare and Sunburst even from a great distance. There were hundreds of horses scattered over the wide meadows. Still Soun never had trouble finding his colt.

Sunburst grew stronger and bigger every day. His long legs became sturdy and sure. He loved to run and play with the other colts and fillies, but he was always careful to keep his mother in sight.

One day Soun came with a buckskin bag with grain in it. The mare was easy to attract to the bag. She ate from the bag while Soun held it out to her. Sunburst, watching every move the boy made, stood behind and off to one side of his mother. His ears were turned forward. His dark eyes concentrated on Soun and the bag he held. Slowly the colt moved closer with his nostrils opening and closing as he sniffed the air. He came almost close enough to touch the bag with his nose. Then suddenly he pulled his head back and galloped away, running in a large circle around Soun and the mare.

This was the beginning of Soun's plan to get the colt to come up to him without being afraid. The boy came every day and did the same thing each time. He always held the grain bag very still. He never made any quick movements. Soon Sunburst was feeding from the bag like his mother did.

That summer the seven-year-old boy spent all his spare time watching the colt feed, romp and play, and grow bigger. Soon Soun was able to stroke the colt's neck while the horse ate from the bag of grain. It was an exciting and happy summer for this Nez Perce boy.

This same summer of 1872 was not a happy one for Young Chief Joseph and the Wallowa Nez Perce leaders. With many more white settlers in the valley came more arguments over who owned stray cattle and horses. To avoid war and bloodshed, Joseph asked the white settlers to meet the Nez Perce leaders in a council on August 14.

Soun watched as the Nez Perce men dressed in their finest outfits. They rode their best horses and sat straight and tall in their saddles. Even the colorfully decorated horses seemed to know that this was a special event. They pranced and threw their heads high as they moved toward the site of the council with the whites.

54

Young Chief Joseph was the first to speak. He stood on one side of the circle of people. He looked at the white settlers sitting on their side. He told the so-ya-po that the Nez Perce were their friends and wanted peace. He said the Indians would not start a war. Chief Joseph talked about the Wallowa Valley and about his promise to his dying father never to sell the land that held his father's bones. He talked long about how the Nez Perce had lived so many summers in the Wallowa that no man could count them. He ended his speech by asking his white friends to take their cattle and horses and leave the valley peacefully.

A Mr. Johnson spoke for the settlers. He told the Indians that the United States government owned the Wallowa and said the settlers had the right to come and take the land. Mr. Johnson said the Nez Perce had sold the Wallowa to the government at the council of 1863.

The Nez Perce argued that they had never sold their land. They said they never signed a treaty selling their valley to anyone. The meeting ended without solving the problem.

One week later the Indian agent, John B. Monteith, came to the valley to speak to Chief Joseph and the Nez Perce leaders. After talking to the Indian leaders, Monteith asked the settlers to come for another meeting.

This time eighty Nez Perce and thirty settlers met in council. Chief Joseph again spoke. He said his father never sold the Wallowa Valley. Someone who did not even live in the valley had signed the treaty. No Wallowa Nez Perce would ever sell his homeland. Joseph used such wise words and spoke so well that even the Indian agent was convinced that the chief was right and the Nez Perce should be allowed to keep the Wallowa Valley as their home.

Soun helped take care of the colorfully decorated horses

while the men talked. He was anxious to get back to the village. He dreamed of the day he would take his first ride on Sunburst. The boy had listened to the words spoken at the council. He could not understand why his people had to give their land to the white man. As Soun listened to his uncle speak the truth, he knew that everything would be all right. This small boy had no way of knowing that nothing said or done by anyone would stop the white man from taking the whole Wallowa Valley from his people.

Adventures with Sunburst

Soun soon forgot about the problem of the coming of the white settlers. He returned to the village with his eyes on the beautiful mountains towering above the valley. Soon he could see the horses scattered over the meadows, grazing in the bright sun.

All summer the boy spent time with Sunburst. It was not long before the big colt would come running to meet Soun as soon as he saw the boy coming. Soun clapped his hands loudly as Sunburst came bounding toward him. When the colt did not see Soun, the boy would clap and Sunburst would hear and come on the run. Soun always had a treat for the colt.

Next the boy trained the colt to stop when he raised his hand over his head. When Sunburst did it right, Soun took his other hand from behind his back and gave the colt a treat. Sunburst liked berries, grain, wild apples, and chokecherries. This was just the beginning of the training of Sunburst, "the horse who obeyed the boy's hands."

The first people to see Soun make his colt come, stop, run in a circle, and do many other things just by using hand signals were amazed. Other horsemen had trained their animals well, but no one ever saw a colt taught so well by a boy so young.

For all the next year the boy who could not speak and his horse, Sunburst, were together at every chance. Sunburst had become a young stallion. Soun trained his horse to get used to a rope first. Then came the bridle. The biggest step would come the first time Soun would lift himself onto Sunburst's back and ride him a short distance. Before that first ride, Soun let the stallion get used to having the boy's arms around his neck and over his back. Sunburst was not at all afraid of his young master, who had grown taller during the last year.

The day the boy decided to ride Sunburst for the first time, Ollokot came to help his son. Soun clapped his hands. Ollokot watched Sunburst raise his head and come running to the boy. As Sunburst came close, Soun raised his hand and the horse stopped instantly. Sunburst lowered his head and pawed the ground with one front hoof. Soun waved his hand in a circle above his own head. Sunburst ran in a circle around the boy, and at a clap of Soun's hands the stallion came right up to his master. The boy gave the clever horse some wild apples and a warm hug.

"Soun Tetoken, you have trained your colt well. Your grandfather would be proud of you. The Great Spirit has

59

given you special power with your horse. Now you will ride the young stallion and teach him even more."

Soun listened proudly as his father spoke. He stood next to Sunburst, rubbing the horse's neck. Carefully the boy slipped the bridle over the stallion's head and fastened it. Then Soun, using his arms, put his weight on the horse's neck and back. He had done these same things many times before. This time he moved his hand to the stallion's mane and hung on as he slipped his leg up. With a smooth push off on his other foot, Soun raised himself onto Sunburst's back for the first time. The boy leaned forward over the young horse's neck and rubbed it gently.

Sunburst raised his head and looked back to see what the boy had done. He blew air from his nostrils and began to prance from side to side. Ollokot was nearby on the big mare. He rode close to Sunburst to quiet him.

Before Soun knew what was happening, the horse broke into a sudden gallop with the boy hanging on to the reins and leaning forward over the stallion's neck. Ollokot rode close to the galloping horse.

As Soun held tightly to the reins, he slowly let one hand move to the horse's neck. He rubbed his hand slowly along the animal's neck. As he did this, the young stallion began to slow his gallop. In only minutes Sunburst went from a gallop to a trot and was soon just prancing in the deep grass.

Soun continued to rub the stallion's neck. The young horse was walking now. When the boy put both hands on Sunburst's neck and rubbed softly, the horse stopped, turned for a look at his young rider, and then began grazing on the grass at his feet.

Soun carefully slid from Sunburst's back. He reached into

a rawhide bag to get a handful of chokecherries for his young horse.

"Well done, my son," called Ollokot. "Your stallion is ready to obey the touch of your hands. Each time you ride him he will learn more. Train him well and he will serve you well."

Ollokot turned and rode off toward the village, leaving an excited boy standing next to the horse he loved. From that time on Soun rode Sunburst every day. He taught the stallion to turn at the touch of his hand. Many times Soun rode without a bridle. At the touch of Soun's feet the clever horse learned to go fast or slow. Slow soft taps with the heels, and Sunburst would walk. Faster and harder taps were the signal to trot. Even faster and harder and the stallion would gallop. For top speed Soun leaned far over the horse's neck while tapping Sunburst's sides as fast as he could.

Soun trained Sunburst to come, to circle, to lie down, to get up, and even to play dead, all with hand signals. He practiced riding the stallion in a special way to stalk up on wild game. Soun would hang on to the long mane and lie far over to one side with a foot dug into the horse's back to keep from sliding off. With most of his body hidden over one side of the horse, Soun would not be seen by animals on the opposite side. This way he could guide his horse close to a deer or elk without being seen.

Soun loved to listen to hunting stories. He was always excited when hunters returned with pack horses carrying elk, moose, deer, or other game. The Nez Perce people also had some cattle they had gotten by trading horses to white people. Still the Indian people used fish and wild game for their main meat supply. Most of all the hunters liked to trade horses for rifles. A few hunters still used bow and arrows, but most game was shot with rifles. The Indian men became expert marksmen with their weapons.

Soun had played with bow and arrows since he was a very small boy. As he got older he learned to make his own bow and arrows. He became a very good shot and won many contests against boys his own age. He even did well against boys older than he.

As soon as Soun could ride Sunburst well, he began to practice hunting skills while riding. Villagers often saw the boy riding slowly toward a bush or a tree. He would be hanging over his horse's neck away from the target, a bush or tree that was a make-believe elk or moose. When he was very close, Soun would spring to an upright position with bow and arrow ready. His shot was quick and true, hitting the target dead center. The boy and his horse amazed all who saw them work together. They often spoke about the boy who "talked" to his horse with his hands and feet.

Hunting stories were often told in the sweathouses as men and boys sat together in the steamy huts. Soun dreamed of the day he would find his first game animal, stalk it, and make the kill. He would return to the village proudly with meat and hide for his people.

The summer of 1873 was especially beautiful in the Wallowa Valley. The winter snows melted slowly, sending a steady supply of water into the lakes and streams in the valley. The water left in the soil kept the grasses growing thick and sweet.

It was a day in late August when Ollokot came to Soun to say words that made him tingle with excitement.

"Soun Tetoken, you ride well. You have learned much since you were a small boy. Soon you will become a man, and the Great Spirit will send a *Wyakin* for your life. Tomorrow hunters will leave for the high mountain valleys to hunt for game. You will come with us to learn the skills of hunting. Listen and watch with great care. Our best hunters will teach you many things that they have learned from great hunters who taught them. Remember, you are to watch and listen. Be sure to do everything our hunters ask of you. I will be proud of my son. My son, you, too, will be a great hunter some day."

Soun could hardly believe his father's words. He felt the thrill of total excitement fill his mind and body. He felt that he could run farther and faster, jump higher, and work harder than ever before. He would start right away to get ready for this adventure. Time passed slowly the rest of the day, and it was hard to sleep that night.

Soun ran to find Sunburst and to get things ready for the ride into the high mountains. Hides would be taken for use in building small sleeping shelters. Dried fish, berries, and roots were packed. Hunters cleaned their rifles. Hunting dances were done around the campfire that night. Soun watched every move of the dancers and heard every beat of the drums. His eyes were wide open and did not miss a thing.

The bright moon moved far across the sky before Soun finally fell asleep that night. The Sun Herald, calling the people to awake to a new day, came by at first light. Soun was up quickly and hurried with his father to the lake for their morning swim. This was a regular practice of the men and boys of the village. Women bathed later in the day.

Soun returned to the fire his mother had built up from buried coals. He warmed himself quickly and ran off to get Sunburst. The majestic stallion came on the run. Soun left the ground and slid onto the back of his faithful horse. He joined three other boys and rode out to round up the other hunters' horses and the animals needed to carry all the supplies.

After the morning meal on that beautiful August day, twelve men and four boys rode away from the village toward the high mountains. The riders rode on a ridge that followed along the east side of Wallowa Lake. Soun rode at the end of the line of riders. He looked down to his right at the clear blue waters of the lake and then up at the high mountain peaks. He had a strange feeling that something special would happen on this, his first hunt for big game.

The trail followed the lakeshore for more than five miles before a wide canyon opened to the left of the riders. A small creek drained this canyon. Ollokot led the hunters across the creek and up into the canyon. The route climbed gradually along the side of the creek through aspen trees and young fir trees that covered the sides of the canyon near the stream. The riders followed Ollokot single file through the trees. Ollokot was following a faint game trail used by wild animals and once in a while by hunters.

In just a short time the hunters were high above the lake. There was more and more loose rock to cross. The horses slowed down and stepped carefully through the rocky places.

Soun watched Sunburst closely. The young stallion was not used to crossing the loose rocks. Soun was glad to be last in line. He knew Sunburst would not be as afraid when he could follow the rest of the horses through the bad spots.

When Ollokot came to another canyon leading off to the right, he made a turn and started toward a high saddle between two mountain ridges. On top the saddle widened to the south and opened into a large meadow. A stream with many beaver ponds filled the center of the meadow. Trees lined the edges of this wide open space. Willow bushes surrounded the creek and ponds. Large aspen groves at the sides of the meadow provided plenty of food for the beaver.

The riders stopped to look at this high meadow. They had already seen lots of signs of moose, elk, and deer. They read the signs carefully. Soun had learned to read these same signs to help him be a good herder. Now he felt the excitement of the hunt. He knew that everything he had learned would help him find game.

The men and boys rode on the east side of the meadow to the far south end. They set up their camp on a level place in the trees just beyond the meadow. Soun and a boy his age made a shelter together. This boy had a Christian name given him by the missionaries at Lapwai. His name was Jonas. He was a good worker. He loved to work hard and play hard. Jonas was always busy doing something.

Jonas liked Soun even though Soun could only speak with sign language. Jonas was bigger and stronger than Soun but still had trouble beating the smaller boy in wrestling contests, foot races, and shooting with bow and arrow. Soun was good at seeing a weakness, at finding a better way to do something, and was quick to take advantage of the other boy's mistakes. Soun was hard to beat in any contest. Jonas liked Soun. They had lots of fun together. Their friendship would grow stronger every year.

A camp was set up. Firewood was gathered and stacked. Beds were made in the shelters. The hunters would leave early each morning in search of game. They would divide into groups of twos and threes. The hunters stayed on the ridges that led through the mountains. From the high ridges they could look down into the valleys and meadows for elk, moose, deer, and bear.

After three days of hunting, the carcasses of two deer and

a large moose were hanging from trees near the camp. Hunting had been slow. In three more days the hunt would end. Soun and his father had not even seen an animal yet.

On the fifth day of the hunt Soun and Ollokot rode far from the camp. They followed a ridge up to a very high valley that was surrounded by snow-covered slopes. They saw signs that many elk had passed this place only minutes before they came.

With quick hand signals Ollokot told Soun to ride along the valley on the right. Ollokot rode left, staying in the willows and spruce trees. Soun knew his job was to send any game from his side of the valley toward his father on the other side. The boy had only bow and arrows. His father had a rifle and was an expert shot. His father would have the better chance at bringing down the speedy elk.

Soun rubbed his hand on the left side of Sunburst's neck. He tapped the horse's sides gently with his heels. The stallion turned right and began walking along the edge of this high valley. Only a short distance away a few snow fields reached to the valley floor. Soun did not notice the snow. His eyes were scanning the meadows for a glimpse of elk.

Soun reached a ridge on the far end of the meadow. He could not see his father. Beyond the ridge he could see into another valley two hundred feet below him. Soun was surprised to hear thunder in the distance. He saw dark clouds rolling in from the southwest. The wind had started to blow steadily.

Soun rode along the ridge in the direction that he thought he would meet his father. Suddenly Sunburst's ears pointed forward. He whinnied softly. Ollokot rode from behind a large boulder. He quickly spoke to Soun with signs telling him that the elk were just below them in the valley. He wanted Soun to ride west down the ridge to the valley below. Ollokot would ride east and south. They would have the elk between them. Soun's heart beat faster. He knew his father needed his help. He would try his best to do his job well.

Only minutes after leaving his father, Soun heard a loud clap of thunder. The wind blew even harder. Soon a cold rain began to pelt horse and rider. The strong wind drove the rain across the ridge. Soun lowered his head as Sunburst continued down the ridge.

Halfway down Soun was startled by a loud cracking sound. The wind had blown a dead tree over. Soon other dead trees and branches came crashing to the ground. The boy stayed away from any dead trees to keep from getting hit.

The wind blew even harder. Now snow was mixed with the rain. Soun was soaked to the skin. Lightning flashed across the cloudy sky, followed by loud claps of thunder. Soun had never been in a storm like this one.

The boy guided his horse to a clump of dense spruce trees. The trees were healthy and strong. Soun stopped next to the trees which blocked the fierce wind and driving rain. He caught his breath and looked around. He shivered. Sunburst's warm body felt good against his legs.

Soun looked into the valley. He saw small meadows here and there surrounded by trees. As his eyes scanned the valley below, he saw something that looked like a large tan rock near a clump of bushes. He looked at the rock for a few seconds, thinking that it seemed quite unusual. His eyes were just leaving the rock when he noticed a movement. It wasn't a rock. It was an elk lying there.

The great animal slowly got up and stood shaking the rain from its body. Soun trembled with excitement. He had found an elk. What he did next would make the difference between success and failure.

The boy saw the large antlers on the elk's head. They were covered with velvet this time of year. Antlers fall from the elk's head in early spring, and the bulls grow a whole new set every summer. The velvet covering the antlers is full of blood vessels carrying food needed for the antlers to grow. The velvet comes off at the end of summer just before the mating season begins in late September.

Soun studied the elk. He studied the route he would have to cover to get close enough for a shot. The noisy storm would help him get close without being noticed by the elk.

The boy rode only a little farther. Quickly he slid from Sunburst's back. He signaled the stallion to stay. Soun began stalking the elk on foot. In his great excitement, he forgot how cold he had been. Now only one thing was on his mind. I must not miss my chance. I must get close enough for a sure shot.

Soun could see the elk grazing near some trees. Then the animal moved behind the trees and out of view. The boy focused on those trees and kept going down the steep hillside. It seemed to take so long to get to the valley floor.

When Soun reached level ground, he hurried toward the trees where he had last seen the elk. I have lost it, he thought. The elk is gone. I must find him. I must.

Soun crossed a small opening. With each step he took and with each minute that passed, he became even more sure that the elk had gotten away. Suddenly the boy stopped. Not sixty feet away he saw the right rear leg and hip of the elk. The animal was standing behind a clump of young spruce trees.

Soun stood frozen in his tracks. He did not have a good shot. From this angle his arrow would only wound the elk, and it would escape easily. The boy could not move closer without being seen. The only thing he could do was wait. He remembered the advice of his father and other great hunters. Wait for the best shot, but do not wait too long or you may get no shot at all.

How long should he wait? What would his father do right now? When will the elk move? Which way will he go? Soun had his bow ready. His best hunting arrow crossed the bow, and he held it ready to draw and shoot. The excited boy waited. His heart raced. He was breathing fast. He tried to calm himself by taking deeper breaths. His eyes never left the elk's rear leg.

Minutes passed. The storm raged on. The wind was carrying Soun's scent away from the elk. The animal did not suspect any danger. Soun waited for what seemed to be a very long time. He had calmed down a little but was still very tense.

As he watched the elk, he saw the leg move and disappear behind the trees. Before Soun could see which way the elk was moving, the animal's huge head and neck came into view from behind the trees. The animal had just turned around. It stood looking ahead, still unaware of danger.

Soun slowly raised his bow, pulling the arrow back as far as possible. The arrow left the bow and traveled to the target only sixty feet away. It was a perfect shot. The elk went down instantly. Just as quickly as the elk fell, it was up again. Soun had a second arrow ready and sent it true to the mark. The elk ran a short way and stopped. The boy ran closer, staying in the trees. His third shot was all that was needed. The elk went down for the last time. Soun was shaking with excitement as he ran to the fallen animal. Soun's throat went dry.

As the shocked boy stood there catching his breath, he knew this was a great moment in his life. Soon he would be a man. His skill as a hunter would provide meat to eat and hides for clothing and shelter for his family. He could not wait to tell his father the good news.

It took a while for Soun to calm down. He realized the storm was still bad. He was separated from his father. His elk needed to be field dressed right away. Before he had only watched as large game animals were cleaned, but he would have to do this on his own. The boy worked as fast as he could. The work kept him from noticing the cold wet weather.

When the field dressing was finished, the boy ran back to get Sunburst. The faithful stallion was right where Soun had left him. They moved off to find Ollokot. Soun knew his father would be very proud of him.

The young Nez Perce boy's thoughts were interrupted by a loud rifle shot ahead of him and to his left. As the boy turned his horse toward the sound, another shot rang out. In only minutes Soun rode into a small meadow where he saw his father kneeling next to a bull elk even larger than his own.

Soun crossed the meadow, slipped from Sunburst's back, and stood looking at his father. A big smile covered the boy's face. His hands moved faster than ever as he told Ollokot his news. He told every detail as quickly as his hands could sign.

"Soun Tetoken, you are a good son. The hunt has been good today. The Great Spirit has given us game. The earth has nourished the animals. You will be a great hunter for your people. Now we have much work to do. The elk must be prepared for the journey back to our camp."

6

The Wyakin

The last days of the hunt were very good. The camp was full of game hanging from crosspoles tied to strong trees. The meat was carefully cut up so it could be packed on horses. Some of the hunters would have to lead their horses loaded with meat and hides.

Jonas was excited about Soun's hunting story. He had Soun tell it to him three times. He asked lots of questions. Soun enjoyed telling about his great adventure.

"Soun, we will have a great feast when we return to our village. The best hunters will be the first to eat your elk meat. And I, Jonas, hope to have a taste, too. The next time we go on a hunt I will stay close to my friend Soun. He will show me how it is done."

71

Jonas's words made Soun feel good. "Jonas, you are my good friend. We shall have many fine hunts together. You, too, could have done what I did. I will be happy to share my elk with you."

Almost as exciting as his hunt was the feast back in the Wallowa. The best hunters of the village were tasting his elk meat. The people marveled at the story of the young boy's success. Soun was going to be only nine years old at summer's end; he would surely be a great hunter when he became a man.

After the feast, Ollokot came over to Soun. "This has been a happy day for you, my son. It has been a proud time for your father. We have talked often about the time of your Wyakin. Soun Tetoken, the time is here. You are ready. I see it in your eyes. I see it in your work. I see it in all that you do. You must begin to prepare yourself tomorrow. The wise old men of our village will help you. Listen to them. Do what they tell you to do. Think only good thoughts. Do only good and kind deeds. Spend much time alone. Ask the Great Spirit to prepare your mind, your body, and your spirit for your time of Wyakin. After another winter, you will be ready to go into the mountains to your place of Wyakin. There you can wait for a vision for your life. Your Wyakin will guide you and help you to live a life full of goodness."

Ollokot's words to Soun were the greatest challenge of his young life. His grandfather had already talked to him about his Wyakin. Soun had heard many talk about this special event in a person's life. He would learn much more before going out of his village to seek his Wyakin. He would be ready to go out alone with no food, no water, and no weapon. He might wait for days without sleep until his vision came. It might come as thunder, as an animal or a bird, or in a

72

vision. Whatever the Wyakin might be for Soun, it would give him powers he never had before. His Wyakin could be called upon to help him at any time during his life.

Soun had already learned many lessons for his life. He learned that the earth was his mother, and did as all good mothers do. It gave him all that he needed. It gave him food, plants and animals on the land and fish in the lakes and streams. It gave him water to drink and to use to clean his body. The earth fed his horses and cattle. Soun was a brother to the animals, the insects, the rocks, and even the snow and rain that watered the earth. The boy felt like a true part of the earth. He would never cut the earth with a plow as the white man did. He would live as his people always had lived.

The summer ended and fall went by quickly. Soun had cleaned his elk hide and stretched it tightly on a willow frame. After the large hide had dried, Soun brain tanned it. The brain was heated in water for a short time. When it was ready, Soun took the brain material and rubbed it into the hide. This would soften the hide forever. Next the elk hide would be made into a beautiful pair of pants and a shirt for Soun, the proud owner.

The boy learned much about the earth, plants, animals, rocks, water, wind, and all things around him. Old men taught him about life. They told him about the past and what life was like when they were boys. Some even remembered the year that Lewis and Clark came to Nez Perce lands. These were the first white men the Indians had ever met. They had never before seen men with white skin and hair growing on their faces.

Soun listened to the old men tell him how he must act when he was out on his Wyakin. "You must find a special place away from everyone, a place to be alone. You will have

74

no food, no water, no shelter, no fire, no weapon, no horse, and nothing to help you. You must sit in one place. Do not move away. Do not sleep. Keep your eyes and ears open and your mind clear."

"Soun, while you are at your place of Wyakin everything will seem new to you. Everything will seem alive and able to move, to speak, and to care about you. Even the rocks will be full of life. Maybe a wild animal or a bird will bring food to you. Accept it as a gift. Maybe the clouds will open and send you water to drink. Maybe you will see bright lights at night when there are no stars or moon."

"Soun, whatever happens, it is your time of Wyakin. It is the time to receive the vision for your life. You will know when your Wyakin has come to you. Then you may return to us. You will never be the same again. Tell no one what your vision is. Keep it in your heart and sing a song of Wyakin to yourself. One day with your hands you can sing your song at a ceremonial fire. We will sing it with you, but we will never know exactly what your true Wyakin is. That is for only you to know and believe."

When October came, Soun became nine years old. He worked hard and learned many things to prepare him for his Wyakin. Young Chief Joseph was happy as his people packed to leave for their winter homes. It looked as if the United States government would let his people keep coming to the Wallowa Valley each summer. They would share the valley with the settlers who were already there. Everyone could live together in peace.

Chief Joseph was wrong. He would not be happy for long. The settlers and the government would not stop until they had taken the whole valley away from the Nez Perce people.

Soun spent much of his time that winter preparing for his Wyakin. He would be ready by summer.

When the Wallowa Nez Perce returned to their valley in 1874, everything seemed the same. There were no new settlers. The mountains, the lake, the flowers, and the meadows were all beautiful. Nothing seemed different, but soon there would be more trouble with the white man.

Soun was eager and ready to go to the mountains for his long-awaited time of Wyakin. When all the work was done and the village settled, the boy left early one morning to ride Sunburst into the moutains. He was searching for a very special place for his time of Wyakin. As he rode into a large canyon, he looked all around the steep slopes. He had to ride carefully to avoid large snowbanks left from winter. High on a grassy slope, Soun stopped Sunburst and looked across the canyon. He saw a ledge high up on the canyon wall. There were steep rockslides on each side of the ledge. There was no snow on this slope that faced south. Soun could see only one way to climb to the ledge. It looked like a perfect place for his time of Wyakin. He had found his place. He would return after his final preparation was completed.

Soun had a last talk with his father, his uncle, and the old men of the village who had prepared him. On a morning before daylight the Nez Perce boy quietly left his lodge and walked out of the village toward the mountains. He was ready. He had prepared himself well. He was excited but not afraid.

His early morning walk into the mountains was a time for Soun to use his eyes to take in all the sights. Every flower, every tree, every mountain ridge, the lake, the creeks, and all the earth seemed more beautiful than ever. This Nez Perce boy was taking a big step toward becoming a man. He knew his Wyakin would change his life forever. He walked bravely toward the high mountain ledge.

When Soun came to the place where he could see the ledge, he crossed through the canyon and over a creek. Carefully he climbed large rocks to a place right beneath the ledge. He found foot and hand holds that he used to climb the last ten feet. He climbed slowly to keep from falling. He was alone, so an injury would be a very serious thing.

Soun lifted his right leg slowly over the front of the ledge and pulled himself up and over. He could see in every direction. He took a deep breath as his eyes took in all the details of this high mountain canyon.

Soun felt good. He had a fine place to be alone. He could sit and think about all he had been taught. He could listen. He could watch. Most of all he could wait for his vision, his Wyakin. The lad sat, legs crossed, his mind and body ready for this life-changing experience.

Soun felt the warmth of the afternoon sun. He paid no attention to time. He thought only good thoughts. All day his eyes searched the canyon in every direction. When the sun dipped behind the mountains, the air started to cool. Birds began to sing their evening songs. Soun watched them fly back and forth. Night was coming.

As it got darker, warm currents of air rose from the valley floor to mix with the cooler air. The birds were still now. The quiet of night came with the darkness. One by one the stars appeared until the sky was full of them. No wind blew. Soun could hear the creek far below as it ran over its rocky path.

Soun did not get sleepy. He looked at the stars and listened to every sound. He thought so much about the people in his village that he didn't feel alone. He thought about each person who helped him. He remembered their words, their kindness, and their smiles. He felt as if each one of them was helping him right now on the ledge.

The change from night to day happened slowly in this mountain canyon. First the sky began to get lighter. The birds started to sing. Slowly light filled the canyon. Trees, rocks, flowers, and all the details of the canyon came into view. Later the sun itself appeared over the ridge to warm the boy. It felt good, but Soun's eyes became heavy. The sleepiness did not last. Soun busied himself by looking at every feature of the canyon.

It was the middle of the morning when Soun first noticed something moving in the bushes on the hillside across the canyon and to his right. He could not tell what it was at first. His eyes stayed fastened to the spot. Then he saw a dark bundle of fur move into the open. It was a black bear cub. Soon the mother bear appeared, followed by a second cub.

Soun was excited. Maybe these animals would become part of his vision. He watched them closely as they wandered along looking for food. While their mother turned over rocks to look for ants and their eggs, the two cubs wrestled with each other in the grass.

Soun enjoyed watching the bears. Often the mother called her cubs to come and eat some ants and eggs. The Indian boy understood the wonderful ways that animals teach their young the lessons for their life. He knew about the fierce love many animals have for their babies and how they will fight and even die to protect them.

Soun was amazed as he watched the bears come closer and closer. Now they were just below his ledge. The mother bear had found a fallen tree full of ants and eggs. She called her cubs and watched as they licked up the contents of the nest. As the cubs ate, the sow suddenly stood up on her hind legs to look around. Then she looked directly up at the boy. Her small dark eyes studied the boy carefully. She was not afraid and seemed to know that Soun would not hurt her cubs. She seemed to understand that he was there not as a hunter but for some other reason. Soun felt as if the bear were saying she knew him and his purpose. She would go on with her hunt for food and the care of her cubs, paying no more attention to the boy.

Soun had been on the ledge so long he lost track of time. His eyes seemed to see more than ever before. His ears heard even the slightest sound. As darkness came to the canyon, he began his second night there. The stars looked brighter than ever. Again the warm currents of air came over him from below. Soun felt hungry and thirsty. Lack of food made it easier to stay awake, and when his thirst increased, Soun did as he was taught. He imagined he was drinking sweet cold water. He swallowed many times. He thought about being satisfied. Slowly his thirst went away.

Soun remembered little of what happened on his third day. There were small birds, a red-tailed hawk, butterflies, and more sunshine. Hunger and thirst came and left. Soun caught himself dozing. His head dropped many times. He dreamed short dreams full of sounds, animals, and faces of friends and family. He dreamed that Sunburst had come to the ledge to take him home. Still Soun did not feel his vision had come.

The third night on the ledge was very dark. Clouds came over the mountains at sundown. They created a spectacular sunset. The colors were brilliant. This night was windy and warm. Soun felt lightheaded from lack of food, water, and sleep. His dizziness made it feel like the ledge was moving away from the mountainside.

As daylight began to creep across the sky, Soun felt the urge to leave his ledge. Something seemed to be telling him to get ready to climb down and leave. He sensed that his time of Wyakin was almost over. I cannot go, he thought. I do not have the vision for my life. Soun remembered his lessons. "You will know when to come home. You will feel it. If you do not have your vision, you can go again another time. When you feel it is time to come back to us, do not wait. Come!"

Slowly Soun rose to his feet to stretch as he had done before. This time he knew he would not sit on this ledge again. He knew it was time to leave.

Suddenly there was a loud rumbling noise to his right. Rocks began to move. Then the large rock field slowly began to slide. In seconds a landslide was underway. The whole mountain seemed to be moving. The noise was deafening. Soun stood and watched as the rockfall reached the canyon floor and sprayed out over the wide slope below him. Dust filled the air along the path of the slide. Then all was quiet.

The surprised boy watched as the dust cleared. Had he left the ledge a few minutes earlier, he would surely have been injured or even killed by falling rock. As he thought about all of this, he saw something move below and at the edge of the slide. Without thinking he started to climb down and make his way toward the spot where he saw the movement. Soun was drawn to this place in a way he could not explain. He just knew he had to get there and see what was moving in the rocks.

Soun worked his way down the steep slope. He was still

weak and lightheaded from his three days and nights on the ledge without food, water, or sleep.

As Soun neared the place where he last saw the movement, he stopped. Nothing anywhere near him moved. Then he heard a whine. He moved toward the sound. Behind a large rock he saw a small animal shivering and crying. Soun reached down and picked up the dust-covered bundle of fur. It was a tiny coyote pup. The little fellow was still stunned from the shock of being in the landslide. He had lost his mother and all his brothers and sisters in the slide.

Soun knew the pup was a special gift and along with the landslide must be part of his Wyakin. It would be many days before the boy would come to understand the full meaning of all that had happened.

Soun could hardly remember walking home. He carried the coyote pup in his arms. He thought about the legend of Coyote and the sea monster. He knew the pup was a gift that would have special meaning for him for the rest of his life.

Soun walked out of the mountains and along the lakeshore to the valley and on to his village. Everyone he passed stopped everything to watch the boy walk by with the coyote pup. They were amazed to see him return from his Wyakin this way and wondered what had happened, but no one asked him a single question. It was for the boy to know. Others could only wonder and guess about the boy, his Wyakin, and the tiny coyote that came back in his arms.

Soun went straight to his friend Jonas. Jonas had a mother dog that had four small puppies. Soun showed his friend the tiny coyote. With sign language he asked if he could put the coyote with the dog's puppies. Jonas said he could, and just as if the mother dog understood, she let the coyote nurse right along with her own babies.

When Soun ate his first food it tasted so good. Cold water tasted even better. Sleep came easily. He was even too tired to dream.

Soun slept many hours. When he finally woke up, he left right away to find his stallion. Sunburst was glad to see Soun and soon things were back to normal, but the boy could not stop thinking about his Wyakin. What was the meaning of the landslide? What did the gift of the coyote pup mean? Why did all this happen? Soun could not get the questions out of his mind. When would the answers come?

Soun's answers would not come soon. Part of the answer would come from the lips of his good uncle, Chief Joseph. He would speak words that would give meaning to the landslide and the coyote pup. For now Soun would just have to wait and wonder.

Soun did his work, rode his horse, and watched his coyote grow. He began to train the smart little pup, teaching him to obey hand signals.

Soun heard there was more trouble with the white settlers. Several times he saw soldiers riding by in small groups. He liked their uniforms and their flags. Soun was warned to stay far from the soldiers and the settlers. He wondered if they would ever leave so things could be as they were before the intruders came.

The days and months passed quickly. Soun spent a lot of time thinking about his Wyakin. Food, water, sleep, and everything about life meant much more to him now. He weaned his coyote away from the mother dog. He trained the coyote to come, to sit, and to stay. He trained him to run at Sunburst's side as they traveled the valley to check on the horses and cattle. The coyote learned quickly and obeyed all of Soun's hand signals.

Soun named the fast-growing coyote Dusty, because he had found him covered with dust. Dusty was full of energy. He could run for hours without getting tired. His coat was thick and beautiful when the villagers packed to leave for their winter homes. Soun was a happy boy and looked forward to the journey to the river valley. There would be lots of time to ride Sunburst and to spend time training Dusty. It would be a good winter for Soun, his stallion, and his new pet.

Dusty's Courage

During the winter Soun trained Dusty to obey many hand signals. The boy and his coyote were together every day. Soun thought about his Wyakin for hours at a time. He kept thinking about the landslide and how close he came to being caught in it. He wondered about the discovery of Dusty, a helpless animal that needed him badly. What did this all mean? Someday he would learn the real answer.

The winter went by quickly for Soun, and the summer of 1875 started out as a happy time. The boy rode his beautiful stallion through the wide meadows of the Wallowa Valley. Dusty was always with them. He roamed in every direction, looking for mice and squirrels to catch. Soun was careful to stay well away from the white settlers and the soldiers on patrol.

Often, after checking on the herd of horses, Soun would ride along Wallowa Lake and into the foothills of the mountains. Soun loved to ride high onto an open ridge and stop to look back at the great valley far below. When Soun found a high meadow filled with sweet green grass for Sunburst, the boy would slide off the stallion's back and let the big horse enjoy grazing on the sweet grass.

Soun would spend his time playing with Dusty in the flower-filled meadow. The boy would hide from the coyote, and then the clever animal would slowly stalk through the deep grass toward the hiding boy. When Dusty got very close, suddenly Soun would jump from his hiding place to scare the stalking coyote. Then the two of them would roll in the grass in a make-believe fight.

One warm summer morning Soun had finished his work and decided to take a ride to a new place in the mountains. His ride took him through some dense groves of trees and over loose rock. Sunburst had learned how to walk over many kinds of bad ground on these adventures with Soun. The horse was becoming very good at keeping his footing on rough mountain slopes. Soun rode Sunburst slowly, letting the horse find the best way over the bad spots. Dusty, with his long nose to the ground, was always running in and out picking up the scents of many wild creatures.

Soun loved to explore new places and to discover hidden canyons and meadows. He always had his bow and a quiver of arrows with him. He carried a knife that had a metal blade. The handle was made of elk antler from his own bull elk. Soun also had some dried meat and biscuits in a hide pouch tied to his waist.

After climbing slowly through the trees and over some loose rock, Soun rode Sunburst out of the trees and into one of the most beautiful high meadows he had ever seen. The meadow was covered with brightly colored flowers. There was a clear blue pond on the west side of the level meadow. A grassy slope beyond the pond led to a rocky knoll above the water. Soun had the feeling that he was the first human to see this beautiful place.

Even in this high mountain meadow it was very warm on this summer day. There was no cool breeze, and the air was muggy. Soun and Dusty walked around the pond and up the rocky slope on the other side; Sunburst grazed nearby. Soun fed Dusty some of his dried meat. As the coyote ate, the boy walked off and hid behind a large boulder. The game of hide and seek began.

Dusty swallowed the last piece of meat and sat sniffing the air. Then he was up with his long pointed nose to the ground, following the scent of Soun's fresh trail. As Dusty got nearer to the boy, the coyote was as close to the ground as he could crouch. Soun, as he had done many times before, jumped up to escape. Soon they would roll and tumble in their make-believe fight.

During their play this time, Soun was running through a rocky area with the coyote right on his heels. The boy headed for a large boulder to jump on to get out of Dusty's reach. There he could tease the coyote and not be caught.

Just as Soun was almost to the boulder his foot hit a loose rock. His ankle twisted, sending him head first to the rocky ground. His head struck a rock so hard that he was knocked unconscious and blood poured from a gash on his head.

Dusty stopped by the fallen boy. He thought it was part of the game until the boy did not move. The coyote, with his tail down, circled Soun. The coyote knew this was not a game. Soun was hurt badly.

Minutes passed. Soun still lay quietly. Blood continued to run from the cut on his head. As Dusty circled his master, the coyote whined softly. Then the coyote lifted his head and turned his ears to pick up a strange sound. He sniffed the muggy air.

Now Dusty could see some movement at the edge of the trees a short distance away. Looking out at the coyote was a large wolf. Soon another wolf came into view. The wolves were hungry and had smelled the blood. They came out of the trees very slowly. Dusty's tail stood out straight. The fur on his neck and back stood up. He raised his upper lip to show his sharp teeth.

The wolves were much bigger than Dusty. They began to move in on the small coyote. They were amazed that Dusty held his ground. Never had they seen a coyote act like this. Slowly the wolves came closer. They could see the fallen boy. The smell of blood drew them nearer and nearer. The larger wolf was now only one leap away from Dusty. The wolves knew they could kill the coyote easily and get to the helpless boy. They didn't know how fiercely this coyote would fight to protect his friend.

Suddenly the larger wolf leaped at Dusty. Just as swiftly the coyote jumped to one side. As the wolf went past, Dusty snapped at the big animal's front leg. The wolf went tumbling over with a long tear on his left shoulder from the coyote's sharp teeth. From behind the second wolf jumped on Dusty, knocking him over. The agile coyote rolled onto his back, sank his teeth into the wolf's stomach, and pushed with his paws. The wolf let out a loud howl.

Before Dusty could get to his feet, the first wolf was on

top of him. He had Dusty by the back leg and hung on, twisting his head from side to side. The other wolf fought to sink its teeth into the coyote's neck for a death hold. Dusty rolled and tossed so the wolf could not reach his neck.

The wolves, busy first with looking for food and then with attacking Dusty, had paid no attention to Sunburst. The stallion, sensing danger, had been restless; now, hearing all the noise, he ran into the center of the fight with his front hooves flying above the wolves' heads. The pair quickly retreated and stood snarling at the stallion. Sunburst made several charges at the wolves. Each time he reared on his hind legs and came down with his front hooves striking near the wolves. Finally the wolves retreated to the protection of the trees.

Dusty lay badly injured. His right hind leg was torn and bleeding. He had a deep cut on his left side which he was trying to lick.

Sunburst moved to Soun's side. He faced the wolves. He pawed the ground and raised his front hooves often to let the wolves know they were in danger if they came near the boy again.

All of this happened in less than fifteen minutes after Soun's fall. The boy was still unconscious and bleeding. While he lay there and while Dusty and Sunburst fought off the wolves, dark rain clouds had moved over the mountains. In minutes a thunderstorm cooled the muggy air. There was even some hail in the storm. The cold rain and hail drenched Soun, and he began to move his head and arms. He opened his eyes and saw the blood. He rubbed his eyes to clear his vision. He knew he was hurt.

Soun raised himself up on one elbow. He saw Sunburst standing nearby. As he sat up, blood rolled down one side of his face. He felt weak and dizzy. He pulled himself over so he could rest against the large boulder. With his right hand, Soun covered the deep cut on his head. He knew he had to stop the bleeding. He pressed very hard on the cut. It burned with pain. He sat there for what seemed to be a very long time before the pressure of his hand stopped the flow of blood. He knew he would have to stay very still until he was sure the cut was not going to start bleeding again.

The rain continued as Soun leaned back against the boulder. Water poured off the huge rock in a steady stream. The boy cupped his hands to catch the water. He drank and drank the refreshing liquid. Dusty and Sunburst had fought off the wolves to save their master's life, and now the rainstorm was doing its part.

The storm passed in thirty minutes. Soun sat very still. He heard Dusty crying but could not see him. It was an hour after his fall that the boy was finally able to lift himself to his feet. He was still weak and dizzy. His legs felt wobbly, and his head throbbed with pain. With his hand he signaled Sunburst to come to him. The big stallion obeyed. Soun reached out and took hold of the bridle, the same one his grandfather had used when he was a boy. Soun held onto the bridle to steady himself and walked slowly toward the sound of Dusty's cries.

On the ground a short distance away the boy saw the coyote lying on his side. Bits of fur from the wolves were scattered on the ground near Dusty. It was then that the boy realized what had happened. He remembered running and falling. The wolves must have attacked while he was unconscious. Dusty and Sunburst had fought to save his life. The rain had come just in time too.

Soun forgot how weak he felt and quickly knelt to help Dusty. The coyote stopped licking his side. His head went to the ground. Soun saw that the cut on the coyote's side had stopped bleeding. He wondered why Dusty did not get up. Then he saw the badly torn hind leg. He suspected that Dusty would never use that leg again.

Soun gently rubbed the coyote's head while he thought how he could best help his brave friend. He knew he would have to stay near him until it was safe to move the injured animal.

Soun built a lean-to shelter over his pet. He made a bed of grass and carefully laid Dusty on it. In the morning he would try to get his friend back to the village. He knew his family would wonder what had happened to him.

Soun stayed awake most of the night. He offered Dusty water and the last of his dried meat. The coyote did not take the meat, but did drink some water. The night passed slowly. Even without much sleep, Soun felt better in the morning.

It was Jonas who first saw Sunburst and Soun come slowly down the open hillside into the valley near the village. Jonas rode out to meet his friend. He saw the cut, caked with dried blood, on Soun's head. He saw Dusty lying in a sling made from Soun's elkhide shirt. Soun's hands were not free, so Jonas had to wait until they got back to the village to have Soun tell his story.

The boys made a comfortable bed for Dusty. Then Soun told Jonas the story of how Dusty and Sunburst had saved his life. He told how the rain and hail were sent to wake him up before he bled to death. Soon the boy had told his story to his father and many others who came by to learn the news.

"The Great Spirit has been good to you, Soun Tetoken. Your animal friends and the rain were given to you by the Great Spirit Chief. They have saved your life so you can live to serve your people. I am happy that my son has returned safely." Ollokot spoke of the dangers of going to the mountains alone and told his son to be more careful from this time on.

Dusty's wounds healed quickly, but his leg would never be the same. It healed crooked and weak. Dusty would always limp badly and never have the full use of the injured leg. Soun kept Dusty close by his side from then on so the village dogs would not pick on him.

Soun's uncle, Young Chief Joseph, did not see the boy much that summer. There was more trouble with the white man. The United States government gave a construction company a permit to build a wagon road right through Indian land. Chief Joseph went to Lapwai to protest, but the government officials would not listen. Agent Monteith told Joseph to bring his people onto the Idaho reservation as soon as possible to avoid trouble.

The chiefs of the free Nez Perce bands had a council to decide what to do next. White Bird, Eagle from the Light, and Too-hool-hool-zote wanted to go to war against the whites. Joseph, Ollokot, and Looking Glass said that war was foolish and could not help anyone. The shamans, medicine men and women with special powers to heal, also advised against war.

The Nez Perce left their beautiful valley that fall of 1875 with troubled hearts.

Journey of Sadness
and Danger

Another winter passed and the spring and summer of 1876 followed. The afternoon of June 23, 1876, was a perfect one. The sun was warm. The grass and wildflowers were fresh and beautiful. A gentle breeze cooled the air just enough. Soun was riding Sunburst toward the village. Dusty limped along at their side. As he neared the village, the boy saw two riders coming slowly from the north. The second rider was leading a horse that had a lifeless form over its saddle. When the riders came closer, Soun could see the body of a man tied to the saddle of the trailing horse. Soun signaled Sunburst to stop and Dusty to sit.

Ollokot had seen the riders, also. He knew something bad

95

had happened and ran out to meet the riders. The men talked quietly while Ollokot went back to look at the body of the young man tied to the horse. Then they all turned and went slowly into the village.

Soun followed the men into the village. People came quickly from every end of the village to find out what had happened. The two young men told everyone the story of the terrible murder of their friend and brother, Wil-haut-yah. Their friend had been shot by three white men. He had done no wrong. He had had no weapon. He had been murdered for no reason at all.

When the people heard the story of these eyewitnesses, many cried out for revenge. Young men shouted words of great hate and anger. "Kill all the whites! Drive the white murderers from our valley!" Women began wailing for the dead man. The village was plunged into confusion.

Soun was frightened at all this. Why did the white men kill Wil-haut-yah? Why do men kill? Why can't all people live in peace? Soun had no answers. His heart was sad and troubled.

Ollokot stood next to his brother, Young Chief Joseph, as the chief spoke to his people. "My people, I too am sad and angry. The murder of our brother is an evil deed. The men who killed must be punished. They are men who have shown us their hate before this. A. B. Finley and the two brothers, Wells and Oren McNall, are evil men. They hate all Indian people without reason. They have caused trouble before. They must pay for this crime. They must pay, but let us not hate all white people. Only some are bad. Many are our friends. The guilty ones are the ones who will be punished."

The villagers listened to young Joseph's words and knew his words were wise counsel. Next Ollokot spoke.

"Listen, my brothers and sisters. We will demand that those guilty of the murder of our good and innocent young brother be punished. We will make sure justice is done, but we must be calm. Let us not murder as these evil men have. This is what they hope we will do so they can kill more. Let us use the white man's own laws to punish the guilty."

The angry young men listened but did not want to wait. They wanted revenge that very day. Most listened and agreed to follow their leaders' words.

In a few days a treaty Nez Perce from Lapwai came to tell Joseph that the Indian agent wanted him to come to talk about the murder. This was the beginning of more talk and more useless promises. Joseph, Ollokot, and other leaders from the Wallowa Nez Perce band made two trips to Lapwai that summer. By September the murderers of Wil-haut-yah still had not been arrested.

Young men and even Chief Joseph were tired of waiting for white man's justice. Soun watched as young warriors painted their faces, arms, and chests. They spoke of revenge. Soun was fascinated by the war paint and the way the young men hurried to leave on their mission of revenge.

When the warriors were ready, they gathered in one place and sat quietly on their horses to listen to Chief Joseph. "Our brother was killed without reason. His blood was spilled in our valley. His body has been returned to our mother earth. The men who have killed him have not been punished. If an Indian kills a white man in white man's country, the white man gives him a trial and punishment. This time white men have killed a Nez Perce in Nez Perce land. Now we will give them a trial and punish them. We will demand a council with the settlers. We will demand the arrest of the guilty men. We will tell all settlers to leave our valley by next Sunday and never return."

Soun was close enough to hear his uncle's words. He knew that this might mean war. He didn't know that things happening far from his valley would change the life of all Wallowa Nez Perce forever. Soun watched as the men rode off. He was reminded of the words his uncle had spoken at Wil-haut-yah's burial.

"Good Nez Perce people, everything on this earth changes. Some changes are good. Some are bad. Sometimes things happen and a life is taken. When a life is lost, there are always those who need our help, who need our love. Let us give that help and love to the family of Wil-haut-yah from this day on."

The words about change, about the loss of life, about those needing help and love kept going through Soun's mind. He remembered his Wyakin and how the landslide killed Dusty's mother. He remembered how he was led to the little bundle of fur and how he took Dusty to care for and to love. Soun thought about those who took him and loved and cared for him.

Now the meaning of his Wyakin was clear. Soun knew his purpose in life would be to help people and animals in any way he could. Soun would let this lesson guide him the rest of his life. This was the same truth that his grandfather, his uncle, his father, and many of the old men had taught him.

There was no war that summer. The murderers left the valley, and the settlers stayed. The murderers were arrested but never punished. The government promised Joseph that five white men would come to listen to his side of the story. These men would be fair and decide on who had the right to live in the Wallowa Valley.

The five men did come, and they did listen. Their decision was heartbreaking. Joseph was told that he and his people would have to leave the Wallowa forever and live on the reservation in Idaho. He was told his people would have a good life there. If they refused to move, they would suffer great harm. They must never return to the Wallowa. They must be on the reservation by April 1, 1877.

Chief Joseph listened to the message brought to him that January. His answer was short and clear.

"The Wallowa belonged to my father. When he died, it was given to me and my people. I will not leave it until I am forced to go."

Everyone in the village on the Imnaha River listened to Joseph's words and repeated them to each other. The idea of losing the Wallowa Valley forever was unbelievable. How could this be? Many said they would die first.

"Soun, I think our warriors should fight the white men who are trying to steal our land." Jonas spoke in an angry voice as he rode next to Soun while they rode out to check the horses.

"My father says many will die if we fight. He says the white man has more warriors and more rifles than all the Indians on earth. He says we will never drive the white man away." Soun's hands moved slowly as he signed.

"Our warriors are brave. Their aim is true. The Wallowa is ours. What will we do to stop them from stealing our valley? Will we just do nothing and let them take it from us?"

"Jonas, I do not have the answer. We must trust our leaders. They will do what is right and best for our people. We must help them all we can."

After Soun finished his message, the two boys rode in

silence. Each one thought about all that was said. They knew there was nothing they could do by themselves to solve the problem.

It was a beautiful day in the middle of May when Soun ran to find his friend Jonas. They had been back in the Wallowa for only a short time.

"Soun, why do you run so fast? Are you trying to win a race?"

"Jonas, my friend, we have much work to do! My father and my uncle have just returned from Lapwai! We are moving to the reservation! We must ride hard to find all the horses and cattle! We must leave in just ten days!"

Jonas watched Soun's hands move faster than ever. He could not believe the message. Leave the Wallowa! Move to the reservation! Take all the animals! Pack everything! Be ready in ten days! Jonas was sure Soun was wrong! This could not be! It was impossible to believe!

"Soun, you cannot mean what your hands say to me! You must be wrong!" said Jonas.

As Jonas finished speaking, a rider passed by telling everyone the same thing. The whole village gathered to hear the bad news from Joseph and Ollokot themselves. Young men cried out for war, but the two brothers spoke against bloodshed. The people listened and agreed to follow the advice of their leaders. Work began immediately to prepare to leave the Wallowa forever.

Soun found Sunburst, and with Dusty running on his three good legs, they went out looking for Jonas. The two boys met and rode off in search of the horses and cattle. For days they rode from dawn to dark across the great valley and into the foothills. The animals were herded into hurriedly built corrals near the village. Even by riding for fifteen hours a day the people could not round up all their stock.

"We will never find all the animals, Soun. We need more time. Why do we have to leave so soon? We have been here for many summers. Why can't we have time to find all our cattle and horses? This is not right!" Jonas spoke in anger. His questions were the same ones being asked by all the Wallowa Nez Perce.

"The white general will not wait. He will come with many men and rifles. He will not listen to our people," answered Soun.

"The great rivers of the valleys below are filled to their banks. How will we ever cross them with our animals? How will the women, children, and old people cross the swift rivers? The white general asks us to do what even he cannot do. Maybe it would be better to die in war," argued Jonas.

The saddest time of all came on a day in late May of 1877. It was the day the people of Chief Joseph said good-by to the Wallowa Valley. They would never return. Sadly the people took time for one last look at the valley they loved. The lake was especially beautiful that day. The root-digging grounds were abloom with new plants. The meadows were green with grass for their herds. Many visited the graves of their dead and stood silently near these sacred sites.

Soun rode his great stallion to the place where Sunburst had been born. He remembered that exciting day as if it had just happened. He rubbed Sunburst's head. He fought back the tears. Soun knew he must be brave. He would do everything he could to help his people reach their new home. There was no time for crying. It would not help.

As the last of the Wallowa Nez Perce rode out of the valley that day, some white men were already looking for horses and cattle that the Indians did not have time to round up. Some of the young warriors had to be stopped from returning to kill the settlers who now took their animals as well as their land.

When the Indians reached the mighty Snake River with all their belongings and animals, it seemed impossible that they could cross without many of them being swept away and drowned. The water was so high and so wild that the roaring noise made it hard for the people to hear each other.

Thousands of horses and cattle and all the men, women, and children milled about by the waters of the raging Snake River. Several brave young men rode their horses right into the powerful current of yellowish-brown water. The riders clung to their mounts as water often poured completely over horse and rider. The braves hung on and dug their heels into the frightened animals' sides. After a long struggle the brave men and their sure-footed horses finally climbed out of the icy water on the opposite bank.

Quickly the people set about making rafts. The work went on for hours. Soun, Jonas, and other boys rode back and forth behind the animals to keep them near the river.

Sunburst stayed calm. Soun rubbed his neck to let him know that everything was all right. Dusty circled them nervously. The coyote knew that great danger was near. Soun slid to the ground several times to pet the coyote and to give him a piece of dried fish.

Suddenly Soun heard a voice shout above all the noise and confusion. "Animals and people nearest the river, rafts packed and ready, begin to cross, now!"

Soun and Jonas watched as rafts were lowered into the water. Three or four horses and their riders towed the loaded craft into the raging current. Old people and small children perched on top of the baggage.

Horses struggled to pull the awkward rafts through the boiling water. The current swept them hundreds of feet downstream as the battle continued. Several riders disappeared completely under the angry water as their mounts lost footing. Each rider hung on and came back up a short way downstream. Amazingly, not a person was lost. All reached the other shore safely.

Next a signal was given to drive some of the horses and cattle into the river. Again Soun and Jonas were told to hold back and care for the rest of the horses and cattle.

It was a long night on the bank of the Snake River. Soun did not sleep much. He was anxious about what he had to do the next day. He had to keep alert to make sure the animals still on his side stayed near the river.

When the first light of morning came, rafts were quickly loaded. Baggage was tied on tightly. Horses and cattle were moved close to the river. Soun and Jonas ate their dried fish while they sat on their horses waiting for their turn to cross the dangerous river.

"Soun, we must ride better than ever before! We are to pull a raft across the angry water! We can do it!" Jonas spoke like someone much older than his twelve summers.

Soun's hands moved quickly as he said, "We will ride as men today. Our faithful horses can make it! We must get our people across safely. We will make it!"

"Soun, we will meet on the other side!"

Jonas rode his horse to the river's edge. Soun was right behind him. Each boy had a braided rope tied around his horse's neck. The rope was loose enough to go around the lower neck. The boys could get one or both of their hands under the rope to hang on while they rode through the wild water. Another rope went from this rope back to the loaded raft. This way the horse could pull the raft along to the other side.

Jonas, Soun, and Ollokot would pull a raft across the river. Dusty was placed on top of the baggage with three people. Two small children and an older woman would hang on tightly for the dangerous trip.

Ollokot went into the water first to be the upstream rider. Jonas was next, with Soun and Sunburst right behind. Near the bank it seemed quite easy. Then the horses swam into the swift water. The water was icy. It splashed over horses and riders. The noise was deafening. The horses were full of fear. They struggled to keep their balance. Each rider held on and urged his horse forward.

The raft was swept downstream and pulled against the struggling horses. Soun was hanging on and urging Sunburst to keep going. He looked back a few times to see Dusty crouched low on the baggage. The people held on and stayed low. Everyone and everything on the raft was drenched again and again.

The horses lost some ground in the river, but kept fighting on. It seemed that they had been in the river a long time when Soun turned to look at his father and Jonas. He saw both of them suddenly reach out as far as they could to grab something going by in front of them. Ollokot waved at Soun and pointed to the water. Soun saw a person's head and arms bobbing in the waves. Neither Jonas nor Ollokot could reach the person.

Quickly Soun gripped the rope around the stallion's neck and jumped into the icy water. With his right hand he reached out as far as he could toward the person being swept past

Sunburst's nose. Water splashed in his eyes and mouth. He coughed and gasped for air. His eyes cleared just in time to see the person go under the waves. Soun reached as far as he could and made a desperate grab. His hand hit something, and he held on with all his strength.

Ollokot saw the boy hanging on to the stallion with one hand and to the woman with the other. Soun's head was under water half of the time. His arms felt as if they were being pulled off his body. He could not hold on much longer.

Ollokot shouted to Jonas to turn his horse more downstream. At the same time Ollokot turned his horse toward Jonas. As they came toward Sunburst, the stallion turned toward Soun. This gave Soun just enough slack to pull himself back up on Sunburst. With one last burst of strength Soun pulled the woman up after him. Now the boy hung on as the three horses fought to reach the bank of the river and safety. People watched as Soun and Sunburst struggled on against the current. Ollokot and Jonas urged their horses forward. When Soun thought he could not hold on any longer, he bit his lip and hung on more tightly.

When the three exhausted horses finally reached shore, the raft came sliding onto the bank. With one leap Dusty was on land. Men were there to hold the raft and to pull the passengers to safety. Sunburst dug his hooves into the sand and rock and came out of the water with Soun and the woman still hanging on. Men helped the two weary riders to the ground.

The woman was cold and in shock. She cried out for the children. Soun, exhausted and shivering, leaned against Sunburst's neck. He looked at his hands. His fingernails were broken and bleeding. He had held on so tightly that he had broken them off himself.

There was no time to rest now. Horses and cattle needed care and baggage had to be unloaded and packed on horses. People and animals were scattered up and down the river for a quarter of a mile. Children were cold and crying. Everyone got ready to move on to the next obstacle, the equally dangerous Salmon River.

War

Soun and Jonas helped round up all the animals and hold them in one place. Dusty stayed close by and began to get dry. Soun slowly dried out and warmed up as he worked. The boys were told to let the animals rest and graze. This gave them a chance to calm down after their wild trip through the swollen river.

Only the horses went on to the Salmon River later that day. A few men and boys stayed behind to watch the cattle. The crossing of the Salmon River was easier without the cattle. It was easier also because everyone knew just what needed to be done. They had a better place to cross the Salmon. Still the river was high and very dangerous.

The crossing of the Salmon River was made in only one day. From this river the people made their way up Rocky Canyon to a high meadow called Split Rocks. Here next to Tolo Lake was an ancient camping place. Several other bands of free Nez Perce people were already camped in the meadow. Like the Wallowa Nez Perce, they were being forced to move to the Idaho reservation. The date was June 2, 1877. The Indians decided to spend their last days of freedom camping together in this favorite place.

After settling down and drying everything out, the Wallowa Nez Perce joined the other bands in having a good time together. They dug roots, played games, raced horses, told stories, and enjoyed dances. It seemed like a regular festival.

As the days passed, the more than six hundred Nez Perce knew their time to be free was getting shorter. Day and night Soun heard men talk about all the bad things the white men had done to their people. They talked about having their land taken, their horses and cattle stolen, and their people wounded or killed. The young men began calling for revenge. They began doing war dances and singing war songs.

This was all very exciting for Soun and Jonas. They had never seen anything like it. But the wilder the young men became, the more the chiefs of all the people spoke against war and for peace. They told the young men that war would mean suffering and death for Indian people. They said that the five Nez Perce bands together had only a few hundred warriors. The white man had thousands of soldiers and would keep fighting until the Indian people were defeated. Many women, children, and old people would suffer and die in a war.

The young men did not listen. Still the talk of war went on each day and into the night. On June 12, many young

warriors met outside the camp. Soun watched as these angry young men painted their bodies with war paint. He heard their hateful cries of revenge and death. The warriors mounted their horses for a war parade through the camp.

Soun ran into the main camp and found Jonas. They stood together and watched as the warriors rode past all the lodges. The braves held their rifles high and chanted songs of war. As the warriors rode near the lodges, one horse stepped into some kouse roots that had been laid out to dry. The horse was ridden by Wah-lit-its and another man. Wah-lit-its's father had been murdered by a white man who was never punished for his crime.

Yellow Grizzly Bear saw what had happened to his wife's kouse roots. He was angry and shouted at Wah-lit-its, "See what you do! Playing like you are brave, you ride over my wife's hard-worked food! If you are so brave, why don't you go kill the white man who killed your father?"

These words stung Wah-lit-its. He stopped his horse, looked back, and shouted at Yellow Grizzly Bear, "You will be sorry for your words."[1]

Wah-lit-its had told his friends that he did not kill Larry Ott, the white who had killed his father, because he did not want other Nez Perce to be killed. Now he wept with anger. He decided he would leave camp the next morning, find Ott, and kill him.

Soun and Jonas talked about all that had happened. No one talked about anything else as the day to go on the reservation came. Soun's mother, Fair Land, was in Joseph's lodge helping the chief's wife give birth to a baby. Ollokot

---

1. Alvin M. Josephy, Jr., *The Nez Perce Indians and the Opening of the Northwest* (New Haven: Yale University Press, 1965), p. 500.

and Joseph were butchering cattle near the Salmon River. The meat would be taken with them onto the reservation.

As the people talked that day, a council was called to decide what to do next. It was then that a man shouted out, "You talk for nothing! Three boys have already started the war! They have killed a white man and have brought his horse to this camp. It is war already!"[2]

It was true. Soun had watched a brave named Swan Necklace ride into camp on the white man's horse. He heard Swan Necklace tell friends how he helped murder four white men who had been guilty of awful crimes against Nez Perce people.

Soun had never heard such words of hate. Since he was a small boy, he had heard his grandfather, his father, his mother, his uncle, and all his people talk about living a good life. They taught the children to help each other, to be fair, and to live in peace with all people. Now the words of hate frightened Soun. What would happen now? He wished that his uncle and his father would return right away.

That day and the next the camp was in confusion. People were scared. They thought that General Oliver O. Howard and his soldiers were coming. They started packing as fast as they could. They ordered the boys to round up all the horses. Then the chiefs said no one could leave yet. Ollokot and Joseph rode into camp with twelve horses loaded with fresh meat. Two Moons shouted to them and told about the murder of the white men.

Soun saw his uncle and father immediately ride through the camp. They called out to the people to stop packing and to wait for the army to come. They said they would tell

2. Ibid., p. 500.

General Howard that only a few did the killing. They said if the people left it would mean war and death for many Nez Perce people.

While Joseph and Ollokot begged the people to wait and not panic, Soun heard young men call his father and uncle cowards. Chief White Bird's followers, who had done most of the killing, shouted at the people to pay no attention to Joseph and Ollokot. They told the women, children, and old men to hurry away to a safer place. They called for all warriors to get ready to fight the white soldiers. The war had begun.

Some of the Nez Perce bands left that afternoon. That night at the camp Chief Joseph was in his tipi when a shot rang out and ripped through his lodge. The gunmen rode away into the darkness. Guards were put on duty for the rest of the night.

In the morning Soun was eating when his uncle and father walked through the camp and told the people to pack everything and break camp. They would go to meet their friends who had already left. Joseph said his heart was sad because of the killings and the cries for war.

Soun hurried to find Sunburst and began to round up the horses. Jonas came riding up to Soun on the hillside above the lake.

"Soun, we are going to war! Our warriors will conquer the white soldiers! We will win! We will return to the Wallowa and live as before!"

Soun listened to Jonas's words. He thought about the words of his friend. There was no smile on Soun's face. With his hands moving slowly, Soun said that he hoped no more people would have to die. He hoped that somehow the white general and the Indian chiefs could make peace. He knew

114

his uncle and his father believed in peace and that war would only mean more suffering and more death.

Jonas rode away to do his work. Soun jumped off Sunburst. He reached down to pet Dusty and give him some dried meat. Soun wondered what would happen next. Life had changed so quickly. Would things ever be the same again? Soun hoped that somehow his wise and good uncle could find a way to stop the killing and the war.

Chief Joseph and the Wallowa Nez Perce joined the rest of the free bands, who welcomed Joseph and his people and told them about more fighting and killing. The Nez Perce camped at White Bird Canyon. The Indian leaders still hoped for a truce and peace talks with the white men.

General Howard had heard about the killings soon after they happened. He sent Captain David Perry and Captain Joel G. Trimble out with one hundred soldiers to protect the settlers. The settlers wanted more than protection. They wanted the Indians tracked down and punished with death. With very little rest the captains marched their troops until they reached White Bird Hill at midnight. When the soldiers reached the top of the hill, they were seen by a Nez Perce guard. He howled like a coyote in the night to warn his people below on White Bird Creek. Then he ran through the darkness down into the canyon to report to the chiefs.

As daylight came, Soun and the other boys were told to drive the horses out of the canyon. Women, children, and old people followed them to safety. The last thing Soun saw was six braves picked to carry a flag of truce to the white soldiers.

Soun and Jonas were moving the herd up an open hillside when they stopped to look back once more. In the morning light they could see the six Nez Perce men walking up the ridge toward the soldiers. One Indian carried a white flag of truce. The boys watched the soldiers ride down toward the six. Without warning the stillness was shattered by the sound of a rifle shot. A soldier had fired at the Nez Perce brave who carried the white flag. At that instant the Battle of White Bird Canyon began.

Soun and Jonas turned their horses uphill to help drive the animals away from the fighting. Women and old men led the pack horses out of sight and out of danger.

The battle in the canyon below lasted only a few minutes. The Nez Perce had the best positions. Indian sharpshooters killed both of the army buglers early in the battle. Now there was no way to signal the soldiers. There was confusion everywhere among the soldiers. Some tried to retreat and were trapped in a blind canyon. At the end of the fighting, thirty-four soldiers lay dead. Three Nez Perce were slightly wounded and none killed. More important to the Indian warriors were the thirty-six rifles and the pistols recovered from the dead and wounded soldiers.

Soun was surprised to see a rider come at top speed out of the canyon. He was shouting to the boys. He told them to turn the horses around and return to the camp. He said the battle was over. The soldiers had been driven away. The Nez Perce had won the fight.

Jonas, smiling broadly, rode by Soun. He called to his friend, "See, our warriors are brave! They are better fighters than any whites! We will win the war!"

Soun did not answer. Many thoughts raced through his mind. He rode Sunburst behind the great herd of horses, driving them back toward the canyon.

Guards were posted around the camp that night. All talk was about the battle and what should be done next. In the

116

darkness Soun carried his blankets out so he could sleep near the horses. Dusty walked along beside him.

It was hard for Soun to sleep. When he did doze, he dreamed. In one dream he was being chased by soldiers. He jumped on Sunburst, who tried to run but could not move his legs at all. The boy woke up often. Each time it was harder to get back to sleep. Soun was a troubled boy.

10

Running and Fighting

The next day, June 18, all the Nez Perce leaders met in council to talk about what to do. They were happy to see a few more warriors come into the camp. These men had been hunting buffalo in Montana. The headmen made a plan that would lead the soldiers on a chase. The Nez Perce people would cross the Salmon River again. They would camp in the high country and watch for the army to come over after them. When the army crossed the river, the Indian people would double back over the river and head for the Clearwater River. All the chiefs agreed on this plan.

Once again Soun, Jonas, and the other boys were riding hard to round up the horses. They headed the large herd back to the Salmon River. At a place called Horseshoe Bend, another struggle against the wild water was made by the people and their horses. The crossing was difficult, but done better than the first two.

Soun was exhausted from lack of sleep and from all the hard work. After getting across the swift Salmon River, the people climbed the steep hills up to a well-hidden campsite on Deer Creek. Soun rode Sunburst along a high ridge above the Salmon River. He could see for miles up and down the river canyon. This was a perfect place for the Nez Perce people to camp and to watch for the army.

From Lapwai, on the Nez Perce Reservation, General Howard and his troops set out to find the Indians. The general had fought in the Civil War and lost his right arm in a battle during that war. He had about four hundred men plus packers and guides. He also took two Gatling guns and a howitzer to use against the Nez Perce.

The high camp on Deer Creek was a fine place for the Indian people. The army did not come to the river for a whole week. Soun rested, played with Dusty, and did his work with the horses. He was rested and thought maybe the army had decided not to fight his people anymore. He was wrong.

On June 27, Nez Perce scouts saw the army on the hills across from the Salmon River. Soun was near the ridge above the river. He rode Sunburst over to a good place to see the army. It scared Soun when he saw all the soldiers. There were so many of them. They all dressed alike and rode in even lines. One carried an American flag. Others carried blue and white flags with numbers on them. Soun could see supply wagons pulled by teams of horses. He even saw the

121

cannon pulled by a team of big horses. Soun stared at this unusual sight for several minutes.

"Soun, let's go! The warrior is waving the red blanket! He tells our people that the soldiers are coming!" Jonas shouted at his friend and the two boys moved their horses at a gallop toward the herd grazing near the camp. Ollokot rode near them to tell the boys that the camp and horses would move that night to an even higher place in the mountains. The new camp would be much farther from the Salmon River and a safe distance from the soldiers.

The boys worked late into the night to move the three thousand horses. They helped set up a camp in the darkness. The next morning the people made their camp more comfortable. Scouts stayed on the ridges above the river to watch the army.

It took four days for General Howard and his men to get ready to cross the dangerous river. The Nez Perce rested, dug kouse roots, and even had time for games and hunting. On June 30 the Indian scouts raced past Soun and Sunburst. "The soldiers are trying to cross the river!" yelled the scouts. "We count more than three hundred soldiers!"

Quickly plans were made and the people all hurried to pack and leave. This time the horses and people would have to travel over rough, steep ridges that led north above the great Salmon River. The horses could not carry all the baggage over this dangerous route. Many valuable things would have to be left behind. Everyone hid their things, hoping to come back for them after the war.

Women, children, old people, and the sick left first on the best horses. The rest of the people, leading the pack horses, followed. Behind them the boys and some warriors moved the herd slowly along. Soun and Jonas rode near each other.

122

The going was slow and difficult. The ridges were steep and rocky. There were no level places. The rock was loose and extremely dangerous. Soon the thousands of horses were spread out in a line more than a mile long. Sunburst had never gone over such a rough trail.

This trip began in the middle of the morning. The horses and people kept going all day and into the night. The darkness made the trail even worse. Soun had been riding Sunburst for thirteen hours. The boy was sore and stiff. The stallion's head drooped. At a short rest stop, Soun caught another horse. He let Sunburst loose and gave him a rest while he rode a fresh horse.

A bright moon appeared and helped a little, but still many horses stumbled and fell. The night seemed to last forever. Finally the eastern sky began to get lighter. Daylight came slowly. The weary people came to a stop and took time for a brief rest and some badly needed food. Soun ached all over. His arms and legs felt so weak. He looked around at all the people. Children were crying, old people sat with their heads nodding in sleepiness, women passed out dried meat and biscuits. There was no time for cooking. Sunburst grazed with the herd. Horses and people enjoyed a long drink from a creek of cool sweet water.

The food and water was delicious. Soun walked as he ate his food. It felt good to stretch his legs and to have his feet on the ground. Ollokot walked over to Soun.

"My son, you have ridden long and hard. We must leave again soon. This food will give you new strength. You have done your work well. Keep going. Do not fall asleep. We will soon be far away from the soldiers. We will find rest then."

Soun moved his hands to tell his father that he could keep

going as long as he had to. He would do his part to help his people escape the soldiers. Soun wondered when the ride would end. He wondered when the war would end. How could they keep ahead of the army with all its soldiers, horses, and rifles? Soun trusted his father and his uncle. They would find a way to end the suffering. Soun did not know how they would do it. He just knew they would somehow.

The ride began again that morning, and the trail was still very steep and dangerous. It was early afternoon. Soun was on Sunburst. The rock was loose, and the trail went down a steep ridge. It happened in an instant. The two horses in front of Sunburst started to slide on the rock. At first it seemed as if they were in slow motion. Then one of the horses fell to its side and rolled over and over down the rock. The second horse went down on its stomach and dug its hooves in to keep from sliding. This horse was able to get up and scramble back to the trail. The animal that tumbled down the rocks was seriously injured. One leg was broken and the horse was cut badly. To end the animal's suffering, a brave shot it with an arrow.

When the sun began to set, the chiefs told everyone to stop. Camp would be made here near the Salmon River. The people had gone two days and one long night without sleep. Now finally they could stop for a night. Soun and Jonas did not even take time to pull grass to make a mattress. They just rolled up in their blankets on the ground and fell asleep instantly.

Soun and Jonas were stiff and sore when they heard the Sun Herald call them to wake up early that next morning. They heard the chiefs say that the scouts had seen the army cross the river and the soldiers were following their trail. Now it was time to move the horses, baggage, and people back to the other side of the Salmon River and travel quickly to the Clearwater River.

The Nez Perce crossed the Salmon River at Craig's Ferry. It was the easiest crossing of all. There wasn't as much baggage and most of the cattle had been lost. The cold water felt good to Soun. From the river everyone climbed a trail to a sagebrush flat where camp was set up. This was not far from Cottonwood, Idaho.

While the Nez Perce were getting far ahead of General Howard, Captain Stephen G. Whipple found Chief Looking Glass and his people at their village close to the present town of Kooskia, Idaho. Chief Looking Glass and his people were not at war. They had vegetable gardens, milk cows, horses, and cattle. They were living in peace and quiet that morning of July 1, a Sunday.

After a white flag was put up and a truce talk started, a citizen volunteer with the soldiers shot a Nez Perce. Immediately the rest of the army began shooting. Men, women, and children all ran for their lives. Some were killed or wounded, and others escaped on horses or by running and hiding. The soldiers came into the village, burned the tipis, trampled the gardens with their horses, and drove the cattle and more than seven hundred horses away.

When the soldiers had finished their senseless attack, Looking Glass and his people returned to their ruined homes to pick up what was left. As Chief Looking Glass stood in the middle of the awful destruction, he told his people that this meant war. They would join the other Nez Perce people and fight the white men who had done this horrible thing to them.

On July 3, Soun was up at daylight and riding Sunburst through the sagebrush fields to round up the horses. He saw a Nez Perce scout called Red Spy standing watch on a ridge above the fields. Soun waved to Red Spy and rode on only a short distance. He stopped quickly as a shot rang out and then another. Soun looked back at Red Spy, who was already on his horse and headed for the camp.

Red Spy had shot at two army scouts coming right toward him. He killed one, but the second scout raced away to tell Captain Whipple that he had found the Nez Perce.

That same day they were attacked by Lieutenant Sevier M. Rains and a dozen soldiers. The young lieutenant was not a wise officer and led his men into a battle they could not win. All of the soldiers died in the short fight.

The next part of the Nez Perce run to freedom would take them between two Idaho towns, Grangeville and Cottonwood. There would be soldiers near each town. This would be a very dangerous day. Fourteen young warriors led by Ollokot would lead the way between the towns. Next would come the horses, followed by the people with the best warriors on each side of them.

On that day Soun heard many shots, and he wondered what was happening. He never saw a soldier all day, and the people passed between the towns and came out on to the prairie.

That night at their camp the warriors came in with their first seriously wounded man. His name was Wees-cula-tat, one of the oldest of all the warriors. He was hurt very badly and died later that night. Wees-cula-tat was the first Nez Perce to die in the war. At the burial of their old friend, Soun heard Joseph tell Ollokot that he was afraid many more of their brothers and sisters would die if peace was not made soon.

Chief Looking Glass and his people joined the rest of the free Nez Perce and now there were even more people and horses for the warriors to protect. They kept moving every day until they reached the south fork of the Clearwater River on July 9. Here the people made a camp next to the river. The horses grazed and rested. The people ate, rested, and even went swimming and played games. Soun and Jonas were dirty and hot. They ran for the river and plunged into the clear warm water. They had a great time. Everything was peaceful and quiet. It seemed the war had been just a bad dream.

On July 11, the second full day at this beautiful spot, one of the guards on a high ridge across the river from the camp began to wave his bright red blanket. The soldiers were coming! Soun and Jonas were swimming when Ollokot shouted at them to get out of the water and head for their horses.

Soun ran to find Sunburst. He found the stallion grazing quietly in the shade of the trees. One loud clap by the boy and the big horse came galloping to his master. Soun quickly placed his grandfather's bridle on Sunburst's head, and then rode bareback to round up the rest of the animals. A loud boom from an army cannon scared the horses and sent them scattering. The shell went far over its target.

This time there were more than five hundred soldiers ready to come down the ridge for the attack. To protect the people, Ollokot, Rainbow, and Five Wounds took only eighty warriors across the river. They rode their best horses and split up, going along every ravine leading to the top of the ridge. The Nez Perce sharpshooters soon pinned the soldiers down on the ridge and held them there. It was a very hot day. The soldiers had no fresh water. It was a miserable day for them.

The Nez Perce people came back to their camp to pack and spend the night.

In the morning the 550 soldiers were still held down by

the 80 Indian warriors. During the day the Nez Perce leaders argued about whether to stay and fight or to leave once again. By afternoon many of the warriors had come back to the camp. The soldiers saw this and sounded a charge. In the Indian camp orders were shouted to the people to leave. Many of their things had to be left behind in their hurry to escape from this army. The soldiers stopped in the camp and picked up many souvenirs left by the fleeing Nez Perce.

All the rest of that day Soun rode hard to help keep the three thousand horses moving along the river. Dusty still limped along on his crooked leg. He had kept up during the whole trip and showed no signs of giving up.

Because the soldiers were coming, the Nez Perce people were on the move again on July 13. Now the trail left the river valley and climbed the steep hillsides. The Nez Perce were on their way to the Weippe Prairie. This was the same trail Soun and his grandfather rode to the root-digging festival the summer before the chief's death.

Soun and Sunburst came onto the beautiful prairie just as the sun was going down. The boy and his stallion were weary from the long ride. They stopped to rest at the top of a small hill. From there Soun watched his people move slowly toward their old campsites. He watched as the huge herd of horses moved into the meadows to feed and to drink from the creek.

Soun slid carefully from his faithful stallion's back. As Sunburst grazed, the boy rubbed the great animal's neck. His mind was full of memories of all the happy times he had had on this wide prairie. He remembered the games, the campfires, the horse races, and all the fun at the root-digging festivals. He remembered the day of the mountain lion's attack on the filly, and the time his father had left the horse

128

race to help the injured man. He remembered his grandfather. If only Grandfather could be here! He would find a way to get the white people and Indian people to stop fighting. Grandfather would be able to get the United States government to let his people return to the Wallowa. Soun stood alone with tears streaming down his face.

11

Lolo to the Bitterroots

At the Weippe on July 15 all the chiefs met in council. Looking Glass was to be the war leader. His plan was chosen as the best one discussed that day. The Nez Perce would leave Idaho and cross the high and rugged Lolo Trail to escape to Montana. The war would be left behind, and the Nez Perce could live in Montana or Canada for a few years. After the years away from Idaho the people could come back a few at a time.

After this council each chief met with his own people. Soun listened as his uncle, Chief Joseph, talked about the plan to leave Idaho. He talked about peace and the end of all the suffering and killing. He still talked about a day when he could lead his brothers and sisters back to the beautiful Wallowa Valley.

The people listened silently. Somehow it was hard to believe that anything would ever be the same again. Chief Joseph said each person would have to be ready to help the sick, the wounded, and the old people. The journey over the Lolo Trail would be long and hard. Everyone would have to be ready to do something extra for those in need.

The next day, July 16, the 750 Nez Perce people, their pack horses, and a herd of almost three thousand other horses left the Weippe Prairie and started up the ridge and onto the Lolo Trail. Seventy-two years before Lewis and Clark had come down this same trail and met some Nez Perce people. The two captains, Sacajawea, and the men of the expedition were sick and starving. It was the Nez Perce Indians who gave the explorers food, helped them make canoes, and took care of their horses for a year. Lewis and Clark promised the Nez Perce peace and cooperation from all white people from that day on.

How had things gone so wrong? Why did the white man come and take the Indian lands? Why did the people who had lived here long before the white man came now have to leave? No one among the Nez Perce that day could understand all that was happening. No one could know what was ahead of them on their search for peace and freedom.

Five warriors were chosen to stay behind to watch for the soldiers. There was a short battle with a few soldiers, but the army did not follow the Nez Perce up the Lolo Trail.

The trip on the trail was not easy. The ridges the trail followed wound in many directions and were steep in many places. There were mountain springs of ice-cold water at

certain places along the trail. These spots were used as camping places.

Soun and his friends had a hard time keeping the horses on the trail. The trees were thick. There was very little good grass for feed. This caused the hungry animals to wander off to find food. The boys were always looking for strays.

After a tiring day on horseback, the boys and men ate their evening meal and then left on foot to go out and push dead trees across the trail. This would make it even harder for the soldiers and their supply wagons to follow the Indians.

Soun and Jonas had fun finding dead and rotted trees standing near the trail. They pushed as hard as they could, rocking each dead tree back and forth until the base finally broke and the tree crashed to the ground. The boys had fun toppling the trees and thinking about how much trouble the downed timber would cause the enemy.

As the long days on the trail passed, the horses became weak and tired. There wasn't enough to eat or time to eat what little was there. Many animals became lame and limped slowly behind the others. Soun had never seen horses suffer like this. He was angry every time he thought about it.

It seemed as though the Lolo Trail would never end. On this rugged trail, Sunburst bruised his right front hoof very badly. Soun stood next to the tired stallion and lifted the leg to see how bad the bruise was. He was frightened by the sight. The hoof had been cut and bruised by a sharp rock. If Sunburst could not keep up, he would have to be left behind. Other horses had already been left. To make them useless to the army, the boys used their knives to cut them in the tender part of their hooves to make them even more lame. These cuts would heal later, but it would be too late to do the army any good. This was much better than having to shoot the helpless animals.

That night Soun did not sleep at all. He and Dusty stayed near Sunburst all night long. Ollokot had found and killed a large fat porcupine near the camp. He did it for his worried son.

"My son, take this fat from the porcupine. Rub it on the stallion's bruised hoof. Do it often. It will help. Tomorrow you can stay behind and move slowly. You can care for your horse. Jonas has promised to work hard to take your place with the herd. You and Sunburst will make it. He will heal quickly."

"Oh! Thank you, Father," signed Soun. "We will not give up! We will see you at the end of the day!"

All night Soun watched the stallion. The weary horse lay down most of the time. The boy gently rubbed the animal fat on the bruised hoof. He asked the Great Spirit to help him. He remembered his Wyakin. Things would happen in his life that would require him to help a person or an animal in need. Now he would do whatever he had to do to help his friend Sunburst.

It was a long night. At first light the people were up and quickly ready to move again. Soun watched closely as the big stallion took his first steps. Sunburst still limped badly. Soun had a sick feeling. He wished he could do something more to help his special horse.

Jonas rode over to Soun and spoke to his worried friend. "Today I will do my work and yours. You stay with Sunburst. He will heal quickly. I will look for you in camp tonight."

Soun thanked Jonas. His words made Soun feel better. Yes, he would be at the camp that night! Nothing would stop him from saving Sunburst!

As the morning went on the boy and the stallion fell farther and farther behind the others. Sunburst limped along slowly as Soun walked by his side. They stopped often to rest. The boy wondered if the army was following. How far behind were the soldiers? What if he and Sunburst did not catch up with the people by dark? They would have to spend the night out alone. He would do it if he had to. If he heard the army coming, he would hide Sunburst and run at top speed to warn his people. Soun's mind was full of thoughts and plans that day. He would be ready for anything.

As he rested in the afternoon, Soun thought he heard someone coming from behind him. He quickly led Sunburst and Dusty into a clump of dense bushes below the trail. From there he watched and listened. He was sure he heard voices. He looked up at the treetops. They were swaying back and forth in the breeze. Dead trees leaning against live ones rubbed up and down the moving trees. They made strange noises. Soun knew from his time of Wyakin that when a person is alone he can hear many sounds that he never hears otherwise.

When Soun was moving again, he came to an open hillside covered with good grass for Sunburst. The boy stood and looked far to the south while his horse grazed. There were rugged mountains as far as he could see. He saw that the sun was low in the western sky. Darkness would be coming soon.

As the three of them moved on, the ridge dipped to a deep saddle. It was very hard for Sunburst to go downhill. Soun led him very slowly onto the saddle between the two high ridges. The sun had just set. By the time they climbed the next ridge it was dark. Soun decided to find a good place to spend the night. They had not caught up with their people.

Suddenly out of the darkness of the trees came the figure of a man. Before Soun could move, the man spoke.

"My son, it is I, your father. You have done well. Our camp is near. We stopped early to rest our animals and to give time for our people to make good beds for the night."

Another voice said, "Come, Soun, we will go to the camp. I have a good place for you and your horse to rest. I have cut some good grass for Sunburst." It was Jonas speaking.

Soun who was so alone and so worried only minutes before now felt a warm feeling come over him. Never before had voices sounded so good. He followed his friend on to the camp. Ollokot stayed on the mountain to take his turn as a guard for the people.

Soun slept off and on that night. Each time he woke up, he took more animal fat and gently rubbed it on Sunburst's sore hoof.

The stallion stayed standing during most of the night. The next day the horse still limped but not as badly as he had the day before. Again Soun led Sunburst slowly along the trail behind the rest of the people and horses.

Early in the next afternoon, Soun led his limping horse along the side of a tree-covered ridge. When they came out onto an open place, the boy was surprised to see the people stopped just below him. When Soun came into the crowd he found out why they had stopped so early. There were soldiers just ahead of them. The scouts came back to tell about a barricade of logs that the soldiers were building across the trail in the valley below. This place was called Woodman's Prairie. The scouts said there were only a few soldiers, who were all staying behind the barricade. The Indian leaders told everyone to make camp. There was plenty of grass for the horses and a good water supply. Soun was happy to stop early. He threw his arms around Sunburst's neck. Then he let the stallion rest and feed while he found Jonas. The two boys helped make beds for the old and the sick.

On July 27 Soun watched as Chief Looking Glass, Chief White Bird, and his Uncle Joseph, carrying a white flag, got on their horses and rode toward the army barricade. From the hillside the boys could see the chiefs ride right up to the soldiers.

The three chiefs talked with Captain Charles C. Rawn for a long time. The chiefs said they wished to pass in peace. They just wanted to go on to Canada. The Indians would go through Montana as they had done many times before to hunt the buffalo. There would be no war and no harm to any people in Montana. Captain Rawn told the chiefs that he could not let them pass until they gave up all their weapons. The Nez Perce said they would talk it over and return the next day.

The second day B. F. Potts, the governor of Montana, came to the barricade to talk to the chiefs. The Nez Perce said they could not give up their weapons. They asked the governor and the captain to let them pass in peace. They would not agree.

On the morning of July 28, Looking Glass had everyone ready to leave very early. Their plan was to go around the barricade through the mountains to the north. They would keep the warriors between the army and the people. The Nez Perce would go on toward freedom.

Sunburst had rested during those days at Woodman's Prairie. Soun had taken good care of him. The big stallion's hoof was much better. He only had a slight limp now. Soun rode another horse that he had trained to obey his hand signals.

He rode near Sunburst as the people and horses began their move past Captain Rawn and his men.

The people moved in silence out of sight of the soldiers. They stayed in a deep gulch that kept them hidden well. When Captain Rawn's scouts saw the Indians escaping, they rode to tell him the news. Forty soldiers were sent up the ridge to stop the Indians. They were too late. Then the soldiers tried to get ahead of the Nez Perce. This did not work either. The Indians had completely fooled the captain and his men. To this day the barricade the soldiers built is called Fort Fizzle. Some settlers called Captain Rawn a "nitwit." Others said he did the right thing by letting the Nez Perce go in peace.

The night of July 28 camp was made in the Bitterroot Valley of Montana near the mouth of Lolo Creek. All through this ninety-mile-long valley there would be plenty of water and grass for the horses. The trail would be easy.

Jonas and Soun were tending the horses near the creek when Jonas started waving at Soun and pointing to the east. Coming right toward them were fifty white men with rifles. At the same time Jonas had started waving a large group of Nez Perce warriors rode up on both sides of the whites. Not a shot was fired. The two groups just sat on their horses and stared at each other in silence.

Looking Glass and the five other chiefs rode up to the leaders of the white settlers. Soun and Jonas came closer and heard Chief Looking Glass greet the whites.

"We have come in peace. We are not at war with the people of Montana. We have left the war in Idaho. We wish to travel in peace to Canada."

The white leaders said they wished for peace, also. They said they would not make war against the Nez Perce people.

139

The talk ended and both groups went on their ways. Maybe peace had really come. Maybe the war was left behind. Jonas and Soun both hoped the suffering and killing were over forever.

The Indians took their time going south down the beautiful Bitterroot Valley. The scouts said that General Howard had not even started over the Lolo Trail yet. Everyone began talking about peace and the end of the fighting. Two nights were spent camping near Stevensville, Montana. The Nez Perce even took time to buy supplies from merchants in the valley. When the Indians did travel, they went about twelve miles a day.

Sunburst's hoof was healed now, and Soun rode with Jonas, watching the horses get rested and well fed. On a beautiful sunny morning Jonas was riding near a channel of the Bitterroot River. He saw a wire fence cross a hill toward the main river. Jonas came over this hill near the fence. Below him he saw a boy kneeling by a colt that was lying on the ground next to the fence. The boy was white and about ten years old. His colt's leg was tangled in the fence. The boy was keeping the animal calm, so it wouldn't hurt itself even more.

Jonas's horse made a noise. The boy turned and saw Jonas above him. A look of great fear came on his face, and he started to run. At the same time the frightened colt began to kick wildly.

"Don't run! I will help! I am a friend!" shouted Jonas. Jonas had learned English at the mission in Lapwai. While he spoke Jonas was jumping from his horse. He ran to help with the struggling colt. As Jonas reached the colt, the boy, who had run a short distance, stopped and turned to watch.

"Come and help. Together we can free your colt!" cried Jonas.

Slowly the boy started back. Just as the boy got near Jonas, he looked up to see Soun riding toward them. The boy stopped, ready to run once again.

"That's my friend! Don't run! He has come to help, too! Don't be afraid!"

Jonas's words calmed the frightened lad. Still he stood back as Soun dropped from Sunburst's back and began helping Jonas. The two Nez Perce boys quickly calmed the small horse.

"Come! Help us! Keep your colt quiet while we free his leg from the wire." Jonas spoke calmly. Slowly the small boy came up and knelt down to hold the colt's head. Soun held the animal's front legs while Jonas worked to free the hind leg. The wire was twisted very tightly around the lower leg and had torn some hide off. The colt kicked his free leg in a struggle to get loose.

Soun quickly grabbed the free leg and held on. Jonas continued to pull on the wire with his bare hands. All three boys concentrated on their work. The small boy was no longer afraid. He saw the two Indian boys doing their best to help his colt. His fear had disappeared.

Jonas, using all his strength, finally gave a pull on the wire. As he pulled he lifted the colt's leg at the same time. It wasn't quite enough. Soun saw Jonas pulling as hard as he could. Soun quickly moved closer and helped Jonas hold the trapped leg up. This allowed Jonas to pull on the wire with both hands. That was all that was needed. The leg came free, and the frightened colt jumped to his feet and trotted away. The three boys were left watching the colt disappear over the small hill.

The boys turned to look at each other. The white lad spoke for the first time.

"Thank you. You saved my colt. I could not have done it without you. My name is John," the boy said in a shaky voice.

"John, your colt will heal. He will be more careful near fences from now on. My name is Jonas. My friend is Soun. We are Nez Perce and come as friends. We want to be friends of all people in Montana. We have left the war in Idaho and come in peace," said Jonas quietly.

"Why did you leave your land? Where will you go? Is the army chasing you?"

John had many questions. Jonas tried to answer them the best he could. The three boys talked for just a short time. John thanked Jonas and Soun again before they parted. John knew these two boys were good and kind. He wondered what would become of them.

12

The Big Hole

The Bitterroot Valley is very narrow at its south end. There the Bitterroot River divides into an east and west fork. The Nez Perce followed the east fork, which runs very close to the steep mountainsides. After passing these narrow places the Indians followed a simple road leading to Lost Trail Pass. Camp was made at a spring where water warmer than one hundred degrees flowed out of the mountainside. A large pool, with rocks and sod for the walls, had been made here. Camp was made early that day. This gave the old people and the wounded time to lie in the warm water.

The trip down the Bitterroot Valley was a wonderful time for the Nez Perce people and their herd of horses. There were no soldiers and no war. Children played games. Roots were dug. Men hunted game. People and animals had time to rest and heal. The war was almost forgotten. Soun was excited to see new places every day. Sunburst was completely healed and well fed once again. Dusty was his old self again and still enjoyed playing with his master.

The road up Lost Trail Pass wound through the trees for six miles. At the top the road followed Trail Creek east toward a wide valley called the Big Hole. Large valleys were often called holes by Indian people. Ross Hole, Pierre's Hole, and Jackson Hole are other famous high moutain valleys.

On August 6, Chief Looking Glass stopped near Trail Creek and picked a beautiful grassy place for the campsite. Everyone found a good place to sleep. Since the Nez Perce had left Idaho they had slept in the open under the stars. As he had done since the war started, Chief Joseph went through the camp to see if the old people had good beds. He checked on all the children and the sick. Chief Joseph spoke for peace in every council with the other leaders. Ollokot was the war leader of the Wallowa band while his brother, Joseph, cared for those in need. Soun's uncle always had his nephew helping him make the old, the sick, and the young more comfortable.

On August 7, the people moved through the high meadows along the creek and out into the Big Hole Valley. Here was an ancient campsite used by many different Indian peoples for hundreds of years. Chief Looking Glass told the people that they would camp here at this beautiful place for two nights. There would be time to cut new tipi poles and time to relax and enjoy themselves. Looking Glass was so sure that the army was not coming that he decided that guards did not need to stand watch. The country for miles around

was wild and unsettled. There were no cities or forts within one hundred miles. The Nez Perce people felt safe and at ease.

The next day was wonderful. The sun was warm. Women and girls dug fresh roots and baked them in underground pits. New tipi poles were cut, and lodges were put up next to the creek. Children played in the shallow creek.

That afternoon Soun and Jonas had finished their work and were wading and taking a bath in the creek near the new tipis. Soun and Jonas splashed each other and had wrestling contests in the shallow creek.

Suddenly Soun stopped playing and stood very still, looking up at the top of the hill that was just north of the camp. He signaled for Jonas to look up at the spot. When Jonas did take a long look, he walked slowly over to Soun. Both boys were sure that four white men were standing near some trees and looking down at the campsite. Then the men disappeared into the grove of trees.

The boys stepped out of the water as if nothing were wrong. They went quickly to Ollokot. Soun's hands moved swiftly to tell his father what they had seen. Jonas told Ollokot the same news when Soun had finished. Ollokot hurried to tell Joseph, and the two men went to Looking Glass. The war chief did not think much of their report.

"We are far from the white soldiers. We have seen none since we passed Captain Rawn on the Lolo. No one has bothered us as we passed through the Bitterroot. We have traveled slowly for ten days. The army could have caught up with us easily by this time. Listen, my friends, the war is behind us. Others have also told me of seeing white men. If they were soldiers they would be hiding or attacking. They

146

are only curious settlers going by this place. Go back to your camp and enjoy our time of rest."

Looking Glass had spoken with a firm voice. The brothers left him. When the warrior Five Wounds came to Chief Looking Glass and said he wanted to take some men on fast horses to go scouting, the war chief became very angry.

"We don't need a scouting party. We don't want a scouting party. A warrior might shoot at the settlers and turn the people of Montana against us as happened in Idaho. There will be no scouting party!"

That night of August 8, campfires sparkled in the clear cool air. Drums played as people sang and danced late into the night. It was wonderful to be free and able to enjoy life once again. Jonas and Soun danced with their friends as they had done in times past. It was very late when the fires were banked for the night, and the Nez Perce families entered their new tipis for a night of restful sleep. The stars were brilliant in the clear sky as quiet settled over the peaceful camp.

While the Nez Perce people slept, Colonel John Gibbon and his men marched silently in the darkness toward the Indian camp in the Big Hole. Colonel Gibbon, with 163 soldiers of the Seventh Infantry and some citizen volunteers, had left Fort Missoula on August 4 and moved down the Bitterroot Valley. At about 2 a.m. on August 9 the soldiers walked right up to the Nez Perce horses grazing on the hill above the camp. The troops stopped and remained silent so they wouldn't disturb the horses. Without a sound the soldiers spread out across the hill to wait for dawn.

Soun was deep in sleep as the sky in the east began to show the first hint of light. On the hillside Colonel Gibbon gave whispered orders along the line of soldiers. They were to slowly and silently begin to move down toward the camp.

At this same time Nata-le-kin, an aged Nez Perce man, mounted his horse and rode slowly out of the camp toward the hill to check on the horses. The old man had poor eyesight and did not see the line of soldiers coming right toward him in the early morning light. Four citizen volunteers raised their rifles and shot Nata-le-kin, killing him instantly.

The shots that killed the old man woke the entire village. Before Soun could get up, rifle shots could be heard everywhere. Bullets tore through the tipis. People were running from their lodges. Many were wounded or killed before they could find a place to hide. The soldiers shot at women, children, and every Nez Perce they saw. The army stormed across the creek right into the camp.

Soun scrambled from the tipi. He heard shouts and screams all around him. The boy dove into some deep grass behind the tipi and crawled on his stomach to the creek. He slid into the water and lay hidden next to the cutbank. He could see flashes of fire from rifles all around him. Soldiers and warriors were running in every direction. The noise was deafening and frightening.

Soun began moving through the cold water next to the bank. He planned to escape the fighting and get to the horses as soon as he could. Soun looked ahead to see his way. Only a few feet away a soldier ran toward the creek bank. He jumped to go over the deep place and land on the other side. Soun reached up as the soldier went right over him. He grabbed the man's ankle, spilling him into the deep pool of water. The soldier's rifle was soaking wet and useless. By the time the man stood up in the waist-deep water, the boy had disappeared around a bend in the creek. He got away just in time.

Soun crawled and swam through the water for a quarter of a mile. He went as fast as he could. He needed to get to the horses and keep them from leaving or being captured by the army. The people would need them if they were to have a chance of escaping. Without the horses, all hope would be lost. He must make it!

Soun's body felt numb from the icy water. He had hit his knee on a rock. Safely away from the camp, the boy pulled himself from the water and hid in the willows. Then he dashed across the bottomland for the hill where he could see most of the Nez Perce horses.

Soun was barefoot, but did not notice the pain as his feet hit the rocks and rough ground. He didn't even realize that his knee had been hurt in the creek. Soun could hear the awful sounds of the battle below. The best sight the boy ever saw was his faithful stallion standing on the hill above him. One clap and the big horse came straight to his master. The boy leaped onto his horse and signaled Sunburst with a touch of his hands and feet to head north away from the battle.

As he neared the main herd, Soun saw a Nez Perce named No Heart driving the horses north near the top of the hill.

"Soun, hurry! Look, the soldiers are coming up the hill! Ride hard! We must keep the horses away from them!" No Heart waved his arm and rode behind the herd with Soun.

The soldiers coming after the horses were suddenly turned back by Nez Perce sharpshooters.

In the camp Nez Perce warriors took positions in the willow bushes and began to turn the soldiers back. Colonel Gibbon himself was shot in the thigh. He signaled the retreat. Slowly the soldiers fought their way back to the hill northwest of the camp. On the hillside in the trees the army dug in to save their lives. The angry Nez Perce warriors followed them and pinned the soldiers down in their makeshift trenches for the rest of the day.

The whole camp was still in a state of confusion after the

awful battle. Many soldiers and many Nez Perce lay dead. Dozens more had been wounded. Women, children, and old people still hid in the bushes. Jonas had stayed in the camp and was now out of hiding and helping with the wounded. He wondered about his friend Soun.

Jonas walked among the tipis. The soldiers had tried to burn some of them, but the morning frost and dampness kept most of them from catching fire. Jonas came around a smoldering tipi and saw two shiny pistols lying next to a fallen soldier. He ran over, quickly picked up the beautiful weapons, and turned to walk away. Jonas did not see the soldier roll over with his rifle aimed right at him. A shot rang out, and the soldier slumped forward.

"Jonas, you foolish boy! Put those pistols down! Get away from here! Go help with the horses! You could have been killed! Our people need you! Go do your work!" shouted Ollokot.

Soun's father had saved Jonas's life. Jonas felt so guilty and foolish. A moment of temptation almost cost him his life. He learned a great lesson at that moment.

Because the soldiers were pinned down, the Nez Perce people slowly came out of hiding. They returned to the camp. Soun returned with No Heart and most of the horses. The dead lay everywhere. Most of the Nez Perce dead were women and children. More than sixty Indian people were killed in the vicious surprise attack. The wounded were sometimes sprawled among the dead. Crying and calls for help could be heard from one end of the camp to the other.

Soun found his mother, Fair Land, lying badly wounded. Every family had lost at least one member.

Chief Joseph took charge of the camp. He asked everyone not injured badly to help those in need. Next he told others to start packing all the belongings on horses. Tipi poles were used to make travois so the badly wounded could be taken away as horses pulled the travois along the ground. Everyone worked hard and quickly for fear more soldiers might come soon. Soun's father, along with the other warriors, kept the army busy all day while the Nez Perce people prepared to escape with their wounded. The dead were quickly buried in shallow graves. It was a sad day for the Nez Perce. The war was not over. Even people from Montana had taken part in the surprise attack at the Big Hole. Once again the Nez Perce were on the run.

While Chief Joseph was leading the Nez Perce families and their wounded away from the battlefield, the warriors were holding Colonel Gibbon and his men down all day. When darkness came, Ollokot and twelve warriors stayed all night to shoot at the soldiers so they couldn't move. The Nez Perce people could rest the night and care for their wounded.

At dawn Ollokot and the twelve brave warriors left the battle and hurried to catch up with their families. Soun saw his father coming across the meadows behind him. Soun's eyes were filled with tears as he told his father that his mother had died during the night. Ollokot's head bowed for a moment. Then his eyes met his son's.

"Your mother has started on her journey to the spirit land. She was a good woman, a good mother. We will remember her love and goodness all the days of our lives. Now, my son, we must go and help our people."

During the next three days the Nez Perce moved slowly along the west side of the Big Hole Valley in the foothills of the Beaverhead Mountains. They cared for their wounded and were on guard for more trouble. The Indians left the Big Hole Valley on August 12 and continued on into Idaho along the Lemhi River. There were several minor battles along the way. General Howard was trying hard to catch up with the Nez Perce, but his men and horses were tiring.

Chief Looking Glass was no longer the Nez Perce war chief. Many of his people blamed him for the disaster at the Big Hole. They said that if Looking Glass had had guards posted, the soldiers never could have made their sneak attack. Poker Joe, a Nez Perce who lived in the Bitterroot Valley, was chosen as the new leader. He knew every trail in Montana and Wyoming.

The Nez Perce crossed Bannock Pass, then traveled over the ridges close to Monida Pass and on to Targhee Pass. Here the Indians followed the Madison River into Yellowstone National Park on August 23.

An Escape and a Miracle

Yellowstone National Park was created in 1872 by the United States Congress. There were only a few simple roads and trails for tourists to follow in 1877. That August 24 Jonas was out looking for some of the Nez Perce horses that had wandered away. He rode to the top of a small hill that was partly covered with spruce trees. From there he could see the Firehole River. When he looked down at this beautiful river, he was surprised to see tents and a campfire. As he studied the scene, he saw three white people walk from behind one of the tents and over to the fire. Jonas didn't make a sound. He turned his horse away and rode quietly in the direction he had come. When he was far enough away, he made his horse gallop back to his people. On the way he met a group of scouts and told them about the white people.

These young men decided that the tourists would be a danger to the Nez Perce people. They could tell the soldiers where the Indians were and which way they were traveling. Minutes later the scouts rode into the tourists' campsite and took them prisoner.

Chief Joseph was unhappy when he found out what the young men had done. Joseph wanted the tourists set free immediately. Some young warriors began to shout, "All whites are our enemies! They attack us in our beds! They kill our women and children! Let us kill these white dogs as they killed our people!"

Soun saw the fear on the faces of the two women and eight men as the warriors called for their deaths. The older Nez Perce leaders said that no one would be killed. They still believed that most white people were good. Only the army was the enemy.

After much arguing and shouting, Poker Joe told the warriors to keep the tourists as prisoners and to not harm them. He ordered everyone to start moving again. More trouble began soon as the line of people and horses spread out for several miles through the forest. Angry young warriors started threatening some of the whites. Two of the tourists escaped into the forest. This made the young Nez Perce wild with anger. They shot two of the men and left them to die. Poker Joe heard the shots and rode back to prevent more trouble. The march continued east.

The next day Poker Joe let the rest of the tourists go free. After a rugged trip through the wilderness, these frightened tourists reached safety. Even the two wounded men were able to recover and return to civilization.

154

Soun was relieved to see the whites set free. All along he wondered how anyone could kill another person. It was the most awful thing he could think of doing. He would never forget the look of fear in the eyes of the helpless tourists.

The Nez Perce scouts knew there were soldiers close behind them. They didn't know that even more armies were moving in to surround them. Troops were blocking the exits from Yellowstone Park. They intended to trap the Indians and were sure that the Nez Perce people would be caught very soon. One of these armies was under the command of Colonel Samuel Sturgis, whose scouts told him that the Clark Fork Canyon was so narrow and rocky that it would be impossible for the Nez Perce to pass through it with all their horses and baggage.

However, Poker Joe had a plan to fool the armies and allow the people to escape again. He ordered the boys herding the horses to drive the animals east toward the Shoshone River. This would make the soldiers think that the Indians would follow that river. When the boys got the horses to a high rocky slope, they were to drive them around and around over many acres, making tracks everywhere. Then they were to turn the horses back toward the Clark Fork Canyon.

Colonel Sturgis's scouts saw the Nez Perce driving their horses toward the Shoshone River. These scouts rode at top speed to tell the colonel the news. Not long after the army scouts rode away, Soun and his friends turned the herd back toward the narrow Clark Fork Canyon.

The canyon would be hard to pass through with all the people and horses. Poker Joe ordered the boys to drive the horses through first. This would help make a trail over the loose rock. Soun was near the front of the herd to keep the lead horses from turning back. At the narrowest part of the canyon several of the first horses through had lost their footing and slid on the loose rock toward the river. The frightened animals scrambled to keep on their feet and dug in to stop their slide. Soun felt sorry for the big animals. He saw nothing he could do to help them except urge them foward to the end of the awful canyon.

Sunburst kept his footing well. As more horses got through the canyon, the route became safer. Most of the loose rock was kicked away and a trail began to appear. The tired people followed with their sick and wounded. Travois carrying the badly injured moved steadily along behind the horses that pulled them on their bumpy journey.

When all had passed through the canyon, Poker Joe put more of his plan into action. Soun, Jonas, and a few other boys joined some warriors to go back into the canyon. Their job was to climb the canyon walls as far as they could and push loose rock across the newly made trail. These rocks would make it difficult for any army to get through and would slow the soldiers down for hours.

Sitting down with his feet against a rock, Soun pushed with all his might. Rock after rock went tumbling into the narrow canyon. He watched each rock go and wished that he could block the way of every soldier forever so his people could go in peace to find their freedom.

With his work done in the canyon, Soun rode Sunburst hard to catch up with his people. Poker Joe's plan had gone as he hoped, although the armies were still very close. The weary Nez Perce moved as fast as they could, not stopping until well after dark. Soun was so tired he nearly fell asleep while riding Sunburst through the chilly darkness. That night the weary boy found a place to sleep behind some sagebrush bushes where he was sheltered from the cold wind. He didn't even notice how hard the ground felt. Soun rolled up in his blankets and fell asleep immediately.

It seemed that he had just gone to sleep when Soun heard his name called. Another day of the awful journey was beginning. The only food left was a little dried meat and some biscuits made from ground roots.

As Soun ate his meager morning meal he began to wonder about the whole idea of the Nez Perce race to freedom. When would this terrible trip end? What would the days ahead be like? Would he and his people ever be safe and free? Would he ever ride Sunburst in the Wallowa Valley again? The questions had no answers. Soun walked slowly out of the camp to find his stallion.

As Sunburst came to his master the boy noticed the stallion's ribs pushing against the horse's sides. The big horse had not had enough to eat for days and days. The whole herd had suffered terribly on the run from the armies. More than a thousand horses had been lost, stolen, or killed in the war. The rest were hungry, tired, and weak. Soun pulled himself onto Sunburst's back and felt the warmth of the stallion's body.

Travel was easier now over gently rolling plains. The cold rain fell hour after hour. Behind the Nez Perce Colonel Sturgis met General Howard and had to tell the general about the Nez Perce people's escape. General Howard was disgusted. Newspapers in the East were already making fun of him and the whole United States Army. Many Easterners were hoping that the Nez Perce people would continue their successful escape.

On September 12, General Howard sent riders with a message for Colonel Nelson A. Miles. He was to leave Fort Keough (near present-day Miles City, Montana) and head off the Nez Perce from the north. In addition, Colonel Sturgis started out early on September 12 and marched sixty miles in the rain to try to catch up with the Indians.

On September 13, Soun was riding with three other boys. They were trying to keep the horses moving along the hills just north of the Yellowstone River. The hungry animals kept stopping to graze. This made it very hard to keep them moving. The route north followed a dry streambed called Canyon Creek. Soun rode to the top of a small hill to drive some stray horses back to the main herd. From the hill Soun looked back toward the Yellowstone River. What he saw startled him. There were hundreds of soldiers coming down the hills toward him.

As Soun turned Sunburst to ride away, he saw even greater danger. Two army scouts were riding out of a stand of trees into the open. They were so close that Soun could see their eyes. The boy was sure the scouts had seen him. He quickly lowered himself over onto the stallion's side. He lay far to one side so it looked like Sunburst had no rider at all. This was the same position Soun used when he stalked elk and deer.

With his hands and feet, the boy signaled the stallion to walk slowly down the hill and away from the two scouts. When they were a safe distance away, Soun quickly pulled himself upright onto the great horse's back. In seconds Sunburst was in a full gallop. The other boys, seeing Soun signal to them, followed. They were riding hard to warn their people of the great danger.

Soun leaned far over Sunburst's neck as he had seen his father do in many horse races. He had the stallion running at full speed. Soon he was far ahead of the other three boys. He rode as hard as he could. Sunburst seemed to know that he needed to go faster than he ever had before. Boy and horse were like one as they raced over the rocky streambed.

Soun kept his eyes moving and searched the hills as he rode at top speed. To his left Soun saw a Nez Perce warrior high on a hill. This man was the guard who carried a red blanket to be used to signal the people when danger was near. The boy quickly turned Sunburst to the left, heading for the base of the hill on which the guard was standing. At the bottom of the hill Soun realized that it was too steep to go up from that side. To ride around would take too long. The boy had to get the guard's attention right away or it would be too late. Many of his people would die!

Suddenly Soun became very dizzy. His mouth went dry. His throat felt tight. Then, with a feeling he had never experienced before, the panic-stricken boy opened his mouth and a miracle happened. He made the first sounds he had made since he was a year old. He called out a warning that would save his people.

"The soldiers are coming! Tell our people! Wave your blanket before it's too late!"

The boy did not understand all that had just happened to him at that frightening moment. It seemed to him that someone else had shouted those words of warning. They could not have come from him, yet there was no one else near. He had spoken! He had given the warning! The guard had heard him. The red blanket was sending out the warning. Now there was time for escape. Now there was time for the warriors to prepare to defend the women, children, and old people.

For several minutes Soun sat motionless on his great stallion's back. He tried hard to understand the meaning of what happened. He thought the same thought over and over. I have spoken aloud! I have a voice! The Great Spirit has given me a great gift, the gift of speaking out loud, a gift given in time to save my people. Slowly the boy leaned forward toward the stallion's ears. He wanted to try speaking again. His throat was still dry and ached with a dull pain. Then he spoke his first words to his faithful horse.

"Sunburst, you're a good horse."

The words were like magic to Soun. He had heard others speak every day, but now he heard his own voice for the first time. It seemed so strange, so different. The boy wanted to speak to everyone right away. He would surprise his father, his friend Jonas, and all the people. Suddenly the magic moment ended as Soun remembered that the soldiers were close by and coming fast.

"Go, Sunburst! Run like the wind! We must help our people escape the soldiers!"

The great stallion's ears were turned back toward the boy. The sound was strange to Sunburst as well. At a nudge of Soun's feet the big horse broke into a full gallop. Three miles ahead was the mouth of a narrow canyon. If the horses and people could enter this canyon, they would be safe again.

Soun rode at top speed toward the main herd of horses. Jonas and other boys were moving them as rapidly as possible toward the mouth of the canyon. When Soun rode past Jonas, Soun shouted to his friend.

"Ride hard, Jonas! We can beat the soldiers!" Soun's voice was loud and clear.

Jonas only glanced toward Soun to see who had yelled at him. Jonas had turned away as if nothing unusual had happened. Then he spun around on his horse to look straight at Soun again. The smile on Jonas's face was the biggest Soun had ever seen.

161

There was no time for words and no time to celebrate. The two boys rode on to do their work. Each of them was sharing the joy and excitement of Soun's great gift. His voice had returned to him after all those years of silence. It was truly a miracle, but now the boys had to ride hard to get the horses safely into the canyon ahead.

The boys soon heard rifle shots behind them. Nez Perce warriors had hidden themselves all along the streambed behind rocks and in low places in the wide channel. The warriors' accurate shots stopped the army immediately. Soun and his friends drove the horses safely into the canyon. The people followed close behind. The warriors held the army down until darkness came and then came into the canyon to join their families. The army did not dare to follow in the darkness. The Nez Perce had escaped once again.

The Indian people moved through the canyon in the dark. It was not a long canyon. It was cold and dark when the families came out of the canyon to make camp on high ground at the other end. The people were weary and cold. There was very little food now. The small children cried as their mothers tried to comfort them. Everyone slept on the hard ground that night.

Nez Perce warriors stood guard all night. Others worked much of the night to block the entrance to this canyon with dead trees, brush, and rocks. Soun let Sunburst rest while he rode another horse back into the canyon to find his father. He had not spoken to anyone since his words to a surprised Jonas. He had talked to Sunburst but only softly. Soun wondered if his voice would stay or if it would leave him. His throat still felt odd.

Ollokot was among the men working in the darkness to barricade the canyon at its narrowest places. Soun slid from the horse he was riding and joined in the work. He said nothing as he worked by his father's side in the darkness. When the moon appeared from behind the clouds, it was easier to see. Soun was helping his father pull a large dead tree over to the barricade. It was very hard to drag the huge tree over the rocky ground. Two boys came to help lift the heavy tree into place on the barricade.

When the tree was in place on the pile, Ollokot turned to Soun and said, "You have worked hard, my son. Now we need rest. We will be moving again before the sun warms the earth. Let us return to the camp."

It was there in the moonlight that Soun raised his hands to speak in signs. Then he let his hands drop to his sides, and the boy spoke his first words to his father.

"Father, today I can speak. Today the Great Spirit gave me a voice. He gave it to me when I needed it to tell the guard to send a warning to our people. Father, I can speak. I have a voice!"

Ollokot stood there in the moonlight with a look of amazement on his tired face. He reached forward and put his hand on his son's shoulder.

"Soun, this is a great day. You are a good son. The Great Spirit has given you a voice to use for your people. I am a happy father with a son who is smiled upon and who has been given many special gifts. You will never forget this day. This is your great day. Now we will help our people find safety and freedom."

The Bear Paws

Poker Joe kept the people moving from dawn to dark for the next two days. The soldiers had to wait for more supplies and fresh horses. This helped the Nez Perce get far ahead of the armies. The warriors were shocked to find Crow and Bannock raiding parties attacking the Nez Perce people and trying to steal their horses. The Crow and Bannock warriors were driven off easily by the Nez Perce marksmen, but it was obvious that peace and freedom would be found only in Canada, more than two hundred miles to the north. If the Nez Perce could make it to Canada, Sitting Bull would be happy to have them join his people there.

On September 17, the Nez Perce people crossed the Musselshell River. They were weary from traveling such long hours every day for more than a month. Many argued for longer rest stops and shorter days on the trail. Nez Perce scouts said the army was now far behind them. More time could be taken for rest. Horses could graze longer. Surely peace was not many days away.

The Nez Perce bands did slow down a little. They did not know that still another army was moving from the east to head them off before they could get to Canada. This army was led by Colonel Nelson A. Miles, who wanted the glory of a victory over the Nez Perce. Colonel Miles was on the way with almost four hundred soldiers and had his men moving as fast as they could go.

On September 21, the Nez Perce camped near present-day Lewistown, Montana. In the next two days they traveled about fifty miles to the Missouri River. Nez Perce buffalo hunters had been here before on hunting trips. They knew the large river could be crossed easily at Cow Island. Steamboats were able to come up river to this point and drop off supplies. Wagon trains took these supplies and delivered them to people living in settlements in Montana and Canada.

Soun was surprised to see large stacks of boxes and bales on the other side of the wide river. There were twelve soldiers and four civilians guarding these supplies. The boys kept the horses quiet while twenty warriors rode their horses across the shallow muddy water of the Missouri River. The warriors stood guard as the signal came for the boys to drive the horses across the river.

The Indians set up camp on Cow Creek two miles north of the Missouri. Several warriors went back to talk to the white men guarding the supplies. The Nez Perce asked these men to sell them food for their hungry families. The sergeant

166

167

in charge said he had orders not to sell the supplies to anyone. The Nez Perce men begged him to help them. The sergeant could only give them some of his own hardtack and one side of bacon.

Back at the camp the Nez Perce warriors were angry because the soldiers refused to sell them food for their starving women and children. When darkness came, the warriors went back and raided the supply depot. They took beans, flour, sugar, rice, and bacon. Chief Joseph spoke against the raid and the stealing, but very few listened to him. Most of the Nez Perce people now believed that all white people were their enemies. In such a war they believed that there was nothing wrong with taking supplies that the people needed so badly.

At the campfire that night, Soun watched almost everyone eat the delicious food. He saw his Uncle Joseph and his father refuse to eat the stolen food. It was hard for a hungry boy to do, but Soun decided he would not eat the food either. Soun stayed true to his teachings. He would always respect his father and never do anything that Ollokot would not like.

The next night Soun was eating a few scraps of dried meat that he had carried for days. He shared some with Dusty, who was now very thin and weak. As the boy ate, he saw the chiefs sit in council around a small campfire. Soun was close enough to hear the angry voice of Chief Looking Glass.

"Our people are tired and hungry! We still move too fast! General Howard is far behind! Poker Joe, you are not even a chief! I am tired of your orders! I am a chief! I will be the leader starting now!"

Poker Joe stared at Looking Glass and answered, "I have done the best I could do. The soldiers have not caught us yet. If we keep going, we will be safe in Canada very soon.

168

You can be the leader, but if we do not hurry, we will be caught and killed!"

Chief Looking Glass had his way. For the next four days the people moved more slowly and stopped every day before dark. Hunters went out and killed buffalo and deer. The fresh meat tasted better than any Soun had ever eaten. He also enjoyed the rest and was glad that Sunburst could take time to eat again. Dusty got his share of meat scraps and was able to catch some mice. There was time to make a bed with grass and weeds. Children were able to rest and even play their favorite games.

September 29 was a cold dark day. The Nez Perce had just passed through the Bear Paw Mountains and were moving across the prairie. The bitter cold wind caused them to shiver as they rode along. At noon the people came to Snake Creek. Hunters had killed some buffalo near this stream. Looking Glass saw the cold and hungry people. He heard the small children crying. The chief ordered everyone to stop. They would make camp in the creek bottom. The bluffs would protect them from the icy wind. There were no trees anywhere near, but dried buffalo manure was all around. These buffalo chips would make good fires.

After taking care of the horses, Jonas and Soun walked down the bluffs and over to the creek. They knew by looking at the sky that it might start snowing soon. Using willow poles, the two boys made a small frame and covered it with hides. It would be a cozy shelter. They helped others with their shelters. Roasting buffalo meat smelled so good. The two boys enjoyed their meal as they sat close to their fire with buffalo robes over their shoulders. While they ate they talked.

"Soun, we are almost to Canada. The war is almost over.

We have only one or two more days of travel. I wonder what it will be like in Canada. Our hunters say there will be plenty of buffalo. We will have good meat and many hides. Our chiefs say we can return to Idaho in a few years," said Jonas with hope in his voice.

"I wish we had never left. War has caused our people suffering and death. How will we ever get back? The soldiers will never let us return. Jonas, our lives will never be the same again. I would give my voice back to the Great Spirit if we could return to the Wallowa in peace."

It was serious talk for these two Nez Perce boys. The camp was quiet and peaceful that afternoon. Most people ate and rested in their shelters. The tired horses, grazing contentedly, stayed close to the camp.

Moving quickly and quietly not far from the Nez Perce camp came Colonel Miles and his army. His men were rested and well armed. The colonel was anxious to find the Nez Perce and win the glory of victory for himself before General Howard and Colonel Sturgis could arrive. Chief Looking Glass knew nothing about this new enemy. He thought all the soldiers were still far behind his people. That night Colonel Miles and his 383 men camped only ten miles from the Nez Perce. He didn't know the Indians were that close.

When Jonas and Soun went to sleep that night, they had no way of knowing that the next day would be the most horrible of all. Soun dreamed that night that he was back in the Wallowa Valley. He was all alone. His voice was gone. White people had taken all the land. He hid but the soldiers found him and chased him. They were almost ready to catch him when he woke.

It was September 30, 1877, another cold and cloudy day. People were up and preparing the morning meal. Hunters

170

were searching for more buffalo. Soon four hunters rode at top speed down the grassy bluff and into the camp. They found Chief Looking Glass and told him that they had seen hundreds of buffalo stampeding across the prairie south of the camp. They all knew this usually meant that soldiers were nearby.

Only minutes after the hunters had talked to Looking Glass, Soun looked up at a bluff and saw a guard waving his red blanket as hard as he could. Others saw the signal, too. People knew that soldiers were coming. They did not know how many or how close they were.

Quickly people started packing. Those already packed started leaving. The horses stampeded away. Nez Perce warriors grabbed their weapons and ran from the creek bottom to the bluffs above. From there they could see hundreds of horses and riders coming straight at them. They hid and waited until the soldiers got closer.

Soun and Jonas and others ran after the stampeding horses. They heard the shooting begin. Soun saw a group of frightened horses circling around wildly. He got a glimpse of Sunburst, his head held high, surrounded by other horses. The boy ran full speed through the sagebrush and grass toward the panic-stricken animals. Suddenly the big stallion saw Soun coming. The boy clapped and shouted. With his hooves flying, Sunburst broke through the herd and galloped to his master. With one leap the boy was on the stallion. Soun knew his job. He must keep the herd near the camp. If the Nez Perce lost their horses, they would lose the battle.

The shooting, the shouting, and the boys running to catch their horses sent the frightened animals galloping in every direction. Soun saw Jonas riding toward a large group of horses. He turned Sunburst in that direction and soon the two boys had these horses moving toward the north end of the camp away from most of the fighting. They raced their horses back and forth, keeping the nervous herd from turning away. It was the hardest riding the boys had ever done, but they were determined to make it back to the camp with these precious horses.

Just when it seemed that the boys would succeed, shots rang out close by and Jonas shouted, "Soldiers!"

These soldiers had been sent to drive the horses away. They would not stop until they did just that. Soun and Jonas were in great danger. Both boys had to turn their horses away and watch as the soldiers chased the herd west away from the camp. There was nothing these two boys could do to stop them. A few Nez Perce warriors shot at the soldiers, but it was too late. The horses were stampeding away permanently.

Soun had lost sight of Jonas and was alone when he saw four soldiers coming toward him. He lay over his stallion's neck and sent his faithful horse into a gallop. The soldiers did not follow, and the boy and his horse rode safely away from the battle. They found a hiding place behind some large boulders and brush. Here they would be safe for a while at least.

From his hiding place, Soun watched the awful battle. Most of the horses had been driven away by the soldiers. Many people made their way through the sagebrush and back down the gentle bluffs into the camp. Nez Perce warriors fought from the edge of the bluffs. When Colonel Miles sent the army charging toward the camp, Indian marksmen killed many soldiers and forced a quick retreat. Soun could see the bodies of many soldiers and warriors in the fields above the camp. There were dead horses and many wounded animals.

Soun knew he had to do something to help. He could not stay hidden much longer. He could ride away and save himself, but this thought never entered his mind. He must get back to the camp with Sunburst. Their help would be needed, but how could he ever make it without getting shot or captured?

Soun searched for a safe route back to the camp. He noticed a shallow gully a short distance away. It looked like this shallow gully might lead to Snake Creek and back to the camp. He couldn't tell for sure. It might be a dead end. He decided he would have to take that chance.

"Sunburst, we need to make it to the gully. Walk slowly. The soldiers will think you are wounded. They will not bother with one horse."

The boy was sure his horse understood. Soun lifted himself onto the stallion's back for the most dangerous ride of his life. After taking a deep breath, the boy lowered himself far to the left side of Sunburst's body. He gave the signal for the big horse to begin walking toward the gully.

From a distance some soldiers did see a single stallion slowly walk across the hillside. They could not see a rider so they continued chasing the main herd. In minutes Soun and Sunburst disappeared into the gully. It wasn't very deep. There were lots of rocks and bushes. The boy dropped to the ground and led his horse through the gully as fast as he could.

The gully made several turns and got deeper. This helped hide the boy and his horse even better. As he led Sunburst around a bend in the gully, Soun came to a sudden stop. There at his feet lay a wounded Nez Perce boy. A bullet had grazed him. His head was bleeding, but he was alive. Soun placed his hands over the wound and stopped the bleeding. It seemed to take a very long time. Sunburst stood quietly waiting for his master's next signal.

Soun rose to his feet and stroked the stallion's neck. He

signaled Sunburst to stand still. Back on his knees, Soun carefully lifted the unconscious boy to an upright position. Soun slid his arms around the boy's waist, maneuvered him onto a large rock, and then stepped onto the rock himself. With all his strength he raised the limp boy onto Sunburst's back. The stallion turned his head slowly to watch. The great horse obeyed and stood perfectly still the whole time.

Soun made sure the boy was safely on Sunburst's back. Then he signaled the stallion to start walking slowly on through the gully. Soun walked right next to the boy to hold him in place. He watched the wound to make sure it did not start bleeding again.

The gully opened up on the creek bottom and the Nez Perce camp. People were digging trenches in the ground to protect their families from the shooting. Many were caring for the wounded. No one paid much attention to Soun as he walked next to Sunburst through the camp.

At the south end of the camp, the boy stopped the stallion and carefully lowered the wounded boy onto a buffalo robe. He used water from the creek to wash the caked blood and dirt from the boy's face and head. The boy began to move a little. Soun told him to lie still and rest. When all the dirt and blood had been washed from the boy's face, Soun recognized him as the grandson of Chief White Bird. He made the injured boy comfortable and gave him some buffalo meat and berries to eat.

The first part of this terrible battle was over when Soun walked through the camp. The warriors were still out on the bluffs in case of another attack. A few shots could be heard now and then but there was a pause in the fighting.

15

A Bitter End

After he was sure that the wounded boy was warm and comfortable, Soun looked around and saw people digging shelters into the banks of the coulees. Some were digging shelters right in the level ground. There was no chance to escape now. The hundreds of soldiers had the camp surrounded. Almost all of the horses were gone. Only Sunburst and a few other horses were in the camp. The rest had been driven off by the army.

Soun was glad to find Jonas digging a cave into the rocky bank of a dried-up creekbed. He joined his friend in the work. They used their knives to dig a large cave. It took them all morning.

175

Just after noon Colonel Miles decided to try one more time to overrun the Nez Perce camp. The Nez Perce warriors heard the thundering hooves of the soldiers' horses and saw the charge coming. The soldiers yelled loudly as they urged their horses on at a full gallop. Again the Nez Perce warriors waited until the soldiers were very close. When the Indian sharpshooters steadied their rifles and fired at close range, many soldiers fell from their horses. Never before had the U.S. Army fought such skillful and tough Indian warriors.

Soun and Jonas had moved Chief White Bird's grandson into their newly dug cave just before this charge began. They watched from inside their shelter and were shocked to see a soldier on a horse come sliding down right over the opening to their cave. This soldier was followed by at least ten more. They had made it all the way into the camp. Warriors on the bluffs above turned and fired at the soldiers, hitting three of them. The rest rode at top speed out of the camp.

This attack cost the lives of many soldiers before Colonel Miles had the bugler sound retreat. The colonel was convinced that the Nez Perce were the best fighters he had ever met in battle. He ordered his men to dig in and keep the Indians surrounded. It would be a long siege.

Nez Perce warriors dug in, also. They watched for another attack, which did not come. In the camp Soun and Jonas helped people dig shelters all afternoon. Both boys' hands were sore and blistered. The weather was cold, damp, and cloudy. The boys were warm while they worked. When they rested, they shivered in the cold air. Little children were crying from fear and cold. The camp was a place full of misery and sadness. The trapped people had little food, not enough blankets, and only a few horses.

When darkness came, snow began to fall. It snowed all

177

night long. Darkness made everything seem even worse. No one slept much. It was too cold, and gunshots could be heard throughout the night.

Soun was sitting next to the injured boy when his Uncle Joseph came looking for him.

"Soun, come close. Sit by your uncle. You have done a great thing today. You have saved a life. You have worked hard to help our people dig safe shelters. You are a man today. Your uncle is proud of you.

"Soun, we have lost many warriors. They have given their lives for their families and for their people. Poker Joe died. Our great old chief, Too-hool-hool-zote, is dead. Many others, even women and children, have died today. My son, you and I have lost much this day. Your father and my brother gave his life for us this morning. He gave his life to keep the charging soldiers out of our camp. You must be brave, Soun. Your father wants you to be a good and brave man. Someday you will take his place. You will grow to be like him. He will be pleased with his son."

The chief stood next to the boy for a few moments, and then left to do what he could to comfort his people.

Soun was numb. He sat staring into the darkness. The words of his uncle seemed like part of a dream. The boy heard them over and over: "Gave his life for us." Soun could not believe it. My uncle must be wrong. When morning comes, my father will be here. He cannot be dead, not my father. Soun's thoughts raced through his mind. He sat motionless. When he stood up, he felt dizzy. He was exhausted. His mouth was dry and his throat felt thick and ached. Tears filled his eyes as he walked slowly back to his shelter. Soun had never felt more alone or more completely hopeless.

Soun was awake all night. After the first shock of hearing

178

about his father's death had passed, Soun remembered the words his father said to him at the burial of the boy's mother in the Big Hole Valley.

"Soun, it is as though part of our own bodies has been cut away. We will never be the same, but we must live on in service to our people. The day will come when we, too, must die. If we die for our people, we die as brave men. The Great Spirit watches over us. He gives us life. Soun, live your life as a good and honorable man. Live each day to serve our people. When death comes, we must be brave." These words came back to Soun as if his father were right there saying them again.

By daylight the snow was five inches deep. The wind had created a blizzard. Soun learned that six warriors had left that night to go to Canada to find Sitting Bull and ask him to come with his Sioux warriors and help the Nez Perce people.

Chief White Bird came for his grandson just after Soun had given the boy some food. The old chief spoke in a steady voice.

"Soun, son of Ollokot, grandson of Tu-ela-kas, you have saved my grandson. The spirits of your father and grandfather are happy with you today. You are brave and kind like them. White Bird will remember what you have done forever. My heart is full of joy because of your good works. You will be an honored one in the band of Chief White Bird from this day on."

The old chief and two of his people helped the injured boy up. Soun watched as they disappeared into the blowing snow. Jonas and Soun worked all morning to help people dig better shelters. At noon the blizzard let up and soon the weather got much better.

179

In the afternoon the Nez Perce warriors heard a voice shout to them, "Colonel Miles would like to see Chief Joseph." These words were shouted again and again. After he met with Looking Glass and White Bird, Chief Joseph rode Sunburst out of the camp for a meeting with Colonel Miles. Two other warriors accompanied Joseph. Looking Glass and White Bird had told Joseph not to surrender, only to find out what the colonel wanted.

At this meeting Joseph and the army officers talked for a long time. The Nez Perce were promised many things if they would surrender. Colonel Miles told them that the next summer they could return to Idaho.

Before the Nez Perce left, Colonel Miles invited Chief Joseph to stay and have coffee. Joseph stayed while Lieutenant Lovell Jerome went back with the other men to the Indian camp. It was then that Looking Glass and White Bird realized the soldiers were holding Chief Joseph as a prisoner of war. Soun saw Chief White Bird grab Jerome's arm while another warrior took the officer's pistol.

"They have taken our chief," shouted an angry warrior. "Let us kill this soldier."

"No!" shouted Yellow Bull. "Give the soldier his gun! Bring him food and water! We will not break the truce as the white man has done! We will get Joseph back!"

Soun watched the next day as his uncle rode back to the camp on Sunburst. Lieutenant Jerome was allowed to return to the soldiers' camp. Every day conditions in the Indian camp became worse. Most of the little children lay cold and hungry in the shelters. Their cries and moans were awful to hear. Joseph went through the camp to help where he could.

During the siege the army began firing artillery shells at the Nez Perce camp. With shells landing in the camp, the

Nez Perce did not dare come out of their shelters. Then a deadly shell made a direct hit on a shelter. A little girl and her grandmother were buried.

On the final day of the Bear Paw Battle one last Nez Perce man would die. The Indians were watching every day to see if Sitting Bull was coming. That morning Chief Looking Glass stood up in a trench to look north toward Canada. At that instant a shot rang out, and the war chief was killed.

By this time the army was stronger than ever. General Howard had arrived with all his men and weapons at dusk on October 4.

In a meeting the next morning Colonel Miles told Chief Joseph that if he surrendered, the Nez Perce people would be taken back to Idaho in the spring. They could spend the winter at Fort Keough where the Tongue River flows into the Yellowstone River. The colonel promised good treatment for all the Indian people.

Chief Joseph returned to tell his people the news. The war was over. They would go back to Idaho the next spring. Chief White Bird said that the white man had lied before. He would not surrender. Chief Joseph knew that without food and warm blankets many women, children, and old people would die soon. Chief Joseph would surrender.

That afternoon Chief Joseph and four braves prepared to go out on to the hillside to tell the general and Colonel Miles that they would surrender. Joseph asked Soun to walk along and be there to hold Sunburst while the leaders talked. The stallion stood quietly as the chief raised himself onto the horse's back.

It took only a few minutes to reach the spot where General Howard and Colonel Miles stood waiting. Chief Joseph rode up to the place and dismounted. His clothes had been torn by bullets. He had bullet scratches on his forehead, his wrist, and his back. He held out his rifle to Colonel Miles, who accepted it from the great chief of the Nez Perce people. All was silent for a few moments. Then Joseph spoke.

"Tell General Howard I know his heart. I am tired of fighting. Our chiefs are dead. Looking Glass is dead. Too-hool-hool-zote is dead. The old men are all dead. He [Ollo-kot] who led the young men is dead. It is cold. We have no blankets. The children are freezing to death. My people, some of them, have run away to the hills and have no blan-kets, no food. No one knows where they are, perhaps freez-ing to death. I want to have time to look for my children and see how many I can find. Maybe I shall find them among the dead. Hear me my chiefs! I am tired. My heart is sick and sad. From where the sun now stands, I will fight no more forever!"[1]

Then Joseph returned to the camp and the people began to come out of their shelters and up to the places where the soldiers had warm fires, hot food, and blankets.

Soun was busy helping people pack when Chief White Bird came to speak to him. "Soun, I have spoken to your uncle. White Bird will not surrender. Tonight I will lead my people through the darkness and escape to Canada. Joseph says you may come with my people if you wish. You can be part of my band, and you will be free."

Soun listened carefully to White Bird's words and an-swered, "Thank you, my great chief. I would be happy with your people, but I have much to do here for my people and friends. I must stay. My heart goes with you and your people."

"Soun, you saved my grandson's life. I shall not forget

1. *Harper's Weekly,* November 17, 1887, quoted by Josephy, p. 609.

your courage and kindness. Now White Bird asks you for one more gift for my grandson. He cannot walk. I would rather die than leave him behind. Will you give him your horse? Will your stallion carry my grandson to freedom? We will return him to you in Idaho someday."

The chief's words made Soun feel weak and confused. Give Sunburst away! Lose the stallion I love so much! He was a gift from my own grandfather! Will I ever see my friend again? Soun could not speak. For several minutes the boy stared at the ground in silence. Then the vision of his Wyakin came back to him. The purpose of his life was to help those in need. He knew what he must do.

Soun looked into the old chief's eyes. He saw there the love of a grandfather for his grandson. He knew the old man's heart. He would give his special stallion to save the chief's grandson.

"Take Sunburst for your grandson. I wish you safe travel. The stallion will serve you well. He is good and strong. He has always obeyed. Take him. He is yours." Soun's words drained his body of most his strength. They were the hardest words and thoughts he had ever had.

Soun did not see Sunburst again. He had to hurry out of the camp with his uncle and his cousin, Sarah. They left just before darkness covered the Bear Paw battleground. It was then that this Nez Perce boy realized that the date was October 5, 1877, his thirteenth birthday. Six years before his grandfather had died. Now his people were surrendering to the United States Army. His whole life had changed in such a short time. It was impossible for a boy as young as Soun to know or understand all that had happened to the Nez Perce people.

On October 6 and 7 General Howard had everyone stay

in camp. Soldiers and Indians rested, cared for the sick and wounded, and prepared to leave for Fort Keough.

During this time Soun spent most of his time alone. He felt miserable. He hadn't seen Dusty in four days. Sunburst was gone. His father was dead. He just wanted to be alone in his sadness. Soun did not even talk to his good friend Jonas.

On October 7, Soun walked down to Snake Creek and wandered through the abandoned camp. It was a lonely place. The snow was melting and the ground was wet and muddy. The boy was deep in thought when he walked near the cave that he and Jonas had shared during the battle. Soun had almost passed the shelter when he saw something move near the opening. He looked just in time to see Dusty come limping out. Soun spun around and scooped the thin coyote up into his arms. He hugged and hugged Dusty, then sat down on a rock to pet the frightened animal. Soun had given up hope of ever seeing Dusty again. For a time the boy forgot how badly he felt about losing his father and his horse. He had his pet back again.

Soun took time to feed Dusty some of his roasted buffalo meat. He spent an hour with the coyote before the two of them walked up out of the creek bottom. When they were getting close to the army camp, the coyote stopped and would not go any farther. Dusty was afraid of these strange people and their large tents. Soun tried to coax the frightened animal on, but it was no use. The boy decided to take the coyote on a walk away from the camp and then return to try again.

This extra walk took Soun and his pet up on a small hill. At the top Soun sat down and fed Dusty some more meat and rubbed the coyote's back. When Soun looked out onto the prairie to the north he saw an animal far away on a hillside. He thought it was a buffalo at first. As the animal moved closer, Soun knew it wasn't a buffalo. It was a lone horse! As the animal came closer, the boy noticed something familiar in its walk. Then Soun realized that it was his faithful stallion, Sunburst. Soun thought it must be a dream. The boy was on his feet in a second and running faster than he ever had before. Dusty was right behind. The big stallion saw the boy and galloped to meet him. Soun threw his arms around the big neck and hugged his friend as tears of joy streamed down his face.

It was really Sunburst! He had returned! But how? Had he run away from White Bird? What had happened? Soun did not know that Sunburst stayed with the old chief until they had reached the Milk River near present-day Chinook, Montana. At this river White Bird and his people met friendly Cree Indians who gave them moccasins and food. White Bird asked them for a horse for his grandson so he could set Sunburst free. This is how the stallion was able to return to his master. Soun had a good reason to smile as he returned to the army camp that afternoon. He lifted Dusty onto the stallion and rode back to his people. He would take up his new life as a prisoner of war. Soun was met by his uncle, Chief Joseph.

"Soun Tetoken, your animal friends love you. Today we are together. Today you and I will work to help our people. They need us. Let us work to make our wounded, our sick, and our old people comfortable. Soun, now you are a man. You have seen more and lived more than most men do in a whole lifetime. You can live a life of service to your people as your father and grandfather did. Together we will return to our mountains next spring. I know you will make the spirits of your father and grandfather proud, Soun Tetoken."

Epilogue

Chief White Bird was right. The white man did not keep his promises. Instead of letting the Nez Perce prisoners return to Idaho the following spring, the Supreme Commander of the United States Army, General William T. Sherman, ordered that the Indians be taken to Kansas. They would be held at Fort Leavenworth. There were 431 Nez Perce prisoners, all forced to live near a hot swampy area. Most were women and children. Many became ill with malaria in Kansas. Twenty-one died before the summer of 1878. Chief Joseph worked hard to convince the government to get his people out of this disease-infested camp. In June of 1879 the Nez Perce survivors finally were moved to Oklahoma. Here disease continued to take its toll. Most of the deaths were among the children. One hundred little ones died.

During the years after the war Colonel Miles did his best to get the government to let the Nez Perce prisoners return to Idaho as he promised they could during the surrender talks at the Bear Paw. Chief Joseph went to Washington many times. He even met with President Rutherford B. Hayes. The chief of the Wallowa Nez Perce worked for years to get his people back to their mountain homes. The Presbyterian church and many individuals took up the cause of the Nez Perce people. By 1883 the whole country was talking about Chief Joseph's cause. In May of 1885, more than seven years after the Nez Perce surrender, 268 Indian prisoners were allowed to leave Oklahoma. Only 118 were allowed to return to Idaho. Chief Joseph and 150 others were forced to go to the Colville Reservation in the State of Washington. During Chief Joseph's years in Nespelem, Washington, he continued to work to get his people back to the Wallowa Valley. He was allowed to visit the valley twice. On one visit he stood silently by his father's grave. Chief Joseph was never allowed to return to live in the Wallowa. On September 21, 1904, Chief Joseph died. The attending doctor reported that the chief died of a broken heart.

Today there is a beautiful Nez Perce Visitors' Center on the Clearwater River near Spalding, Idaho. It is operated by the National Park Service. It is a place dedicated to keeping the Nez Perce history alive. Many interpretive signs mark the historic sites of the war of 1877. At the Big Hole Battlefield the National Park Service maintains a large Visitors' Center and interpretive trails in the Nez Perce campsite area and in the siege area.

The 750 Nez Perce people engaged in a running fight that

189

covered 1,700 miles. The Nez Perce had women, children, sick, wounded, and old people, all their baggage, and thousands of horses. They fought 13 battles with about two thousand soldiers and volunteers. One hundred twenty Nez Perce people were killed during the war. Half were women and children. One hundred eighty whites died and 150 were wounded. Two hundred thirty-three Nez Perce escaped the Bear Paw battlefield and most of them, including Chief White Bird, arrived safely in Canada.

Even the casual reader of this period of Nez Perce history will see that there were many opportunities to avoid this senseless war. On June 17 at White Bird Canyon, Arthur Chapman fired at the six Nez Perce carrying a flag of truce. On July 1 Captain Whipple attacked Looking Glass and his people without reason. Later that month Captain Rawn talked about peace and surrender. When the Nez Perce entered Montana, they demonstrated that they wanted to pass peacefully on to Canada.

There were many chances for peace, many chances to end the suffering for the Nez Perce people. Unfortunately there were no white statesmen great enough to act in the interest of decency and human rights. The United States Army, still smarting from Custer's massacre at the Little Bighorn in 1876, used the Nez Perce people to salvage their "honor." The newspapers of the day added fuel to the selfish hatred of many white opportunists in the Northwest.

Today the Nez Perce people remain proud of their past. Differences between the treaty and nontreaty Nez Perce are mending as the years go by. The Nez Perce remain a highly respected nation of native Americans. They have gone on to defend the United States against enemies of our freedom. They have earned our respect and admiration.